HOW TO
OUTNEGOTIATE
ANYONE

HOW TO
OUTNEGOTIATE
ANYONE
(Even a Car Dealer!)

by
LEO REILLY

ADAMS MEDIA CORPORATION
Avon, Massachusetts

Published by
Adams Media, an F+W Publications Company
57 Littlefield Street, Avon, MA 02322. U.S.A.

ISBN: 1-55850-283-1

Printed in Canada.

T S R Q P O N M L

Library of Congress Cataloging-in-Publication Data
Reilly, Leo.
    How to outnegotiate anyone, even a car dealer! / by Leo Reilly.
        p.   cm.
    Includes index.
    ISBN 1-55850-283-1
    1. Negotiation in business. I. Title. II. Title: How to outnegotiate anyone, even
a car dealer!
    HD58.6.R45   1993
    302.3—dc20   93-34576
                                                                            CIP

This publication is designed to provide accurate and authoritative information with
regard to the subject matter covered. It is sold with the understanding that the pub-
lisher is not engaged in rendering legal, accounting, or other professional advice. If
legal advice or other expert assistance is required, the services of a competent professional person should be sought.
        — From a *Declaration of Principles* jointly adopted by a Committee of the
        American Bar Association and a Committee of Publishers and Associations

A Note on the Personal Pronoun.
To avoid sexism without resorting to such tiresome constructions as *he/she*, *his or
hers*, and so on, I have used the masculine and feminine pronouns aribitrarily
throughout this book, with about as many *hes* as *shes*.

This book is available at quantity discounts for bulk purchases.
For information, call 1-800-872-5627.

Visit our home page at http://www.adamsmedia.com

To Faith, who has patiently endured my company for the
past 15 years with good humor, grace under fire and a
remarkable ability to ignore the cloud
for the silver lining.

Contents

I would like to make a toast and give a tip of the hat to all of the people who have helped in one way or another, to make this book possible. They know who they are but it doesn't hurt to name them anyway. I would like to give a special thanks to my associate Nancy Mickulich, who has helped me in ways she will never know to get this book out, my booking agents, Sue Smith and Margaret Kamamlian, who kept me in clover while I was writing the manuscript, Steve Mandel who unwittingly became a central turning point in my life and has always been a valued friend, my agent Frank Weimann of the Literary Group, my editor Brandon Toropov who gave me encouragement and guidance, not to mention a badly needed prod from time to time, and Kathleen Becker who cleaned up my tortured prose. I would also like to thank my two beloved children Emily and David for being a source of inspiration to me and for keeping their chocolate covered sticky hands away from the manuscript for what must have seemed an eternity. Final thanks must go to my stockbroker and friend of 25 years, Mr. Brad Baker, for injecting a sense of humor when it was most needed.

Introduction

Why You Should Never Take a "Win-Win" Negotiating Book onto a Car Lot

For 15 years, it was my job to negotiate for people. As a trial lawyer, I negotiated everything from the selling price of a business, to the payment plans a debtor would undertake in bankruptcy. I negotiated the mergers of businesses, the dissolution of partnerships, and how much audited taxpayers would pay to the IRS. And, like almost every lawyer or businessperson I have ever met, I did this with no formal instruction on how to negotiate. My entire experience was basically limited to trial-and-error and an occasional seminar that tended to raise more questions than it answered. Negotiating is a fundamental business skill, yet most of us are ignorant of how to handle the most basic negotiations. Even people who are known as professional negotiators are usually just as ignorant of the process. The negotiations between Eastern Airlines and the mechanics union (discussed in chapter 3) prove that even the most tested and experienced negotiators can make mistakes with disastrous consequences, mistakes that were easy to avoid but embarrassingly predictable. Today, largely because of these mistakes, Eastern Airlines no longer exists and the airline's mechanics have lost their jobs.

The fact is, Americans do not know how to negotiate. This is especially true when it comes to bargaining the price and terms of a product, whether the parties involved are well-paid businesspersons running corporations or homeowners negotiating the sale of their residence. Our inability to effectively bargain is not the result of our being less intelligent as the Japanese or less street smart as the Iranians, as some would have us believe. Rather, it is the result of a basic condition.

Americans, more than any other people in the world, live in a highly industrialized consumer-oriented society. Other nations may be richer than us (on a per capita basis Kuwait, Oman, Bahrain, and a dozen other oil-rich nations are wealthier), or more industrialized (Japan's infrastructure is arguably superior to ours in many respects), but no other nation is so thoroughly oriented to the consumer, or has been for such a long period of time. We have the luxury of being able to purchase standardized goods at standardized prices. In fact, the hallmark of a highly industrialized society is this push to standardize everything. For example, if you walk into a grocery store to purchase a box of corn flakes, you will notice that all brands come in similarly sized boxes, and their quality is fairly consistent. Furthermore, when you check their various prices, you will notice they are all priced within a narrow price range. So when you get to the check-out, the price is non-negotiable, because there is really nothing left to negotiate. The price and quality of this product (along with its package size and bulk weight) have already been negotiated for you at the manufacturing and distribution levels.

The advantages of not having to constantly negotiate price in a modern industrialized society are substantial: First, because we purchase products in a free enterprise economy that rewards competition, we are able to get the best products at the best price the market will bear. The price we pay is not determined by our skill as a negotiator. Second, we need not spend time participating in the negotiating process. We are able to simply purchase the goods we want and go home to do other things we find more rewarding or interesting.

The major disadvantage, however, is that when we do need to negotiate a price we don't know how. Only in highly developed societies do we find that most people are uncomfortable with the negotiating process and are anxious to get it over with as quickly as possible.

Contrast this with someone who lives in a lesser developed society. While I lived in London, I had a friend named Peter who was Nigerian. Peter used to tell me stories about his family life in a small village located several hours outside of Lagos, Nigeria. Once a month, they would all go to market to sell the produce or livestock they had raised and, at the same time, purchase provisions to live on. At the agrarian marketplace, everything is negotiable—produce, clothing or fabric, furniture, jewelry, and livestock—because the buyer is purchasing each item directly from the manufacturer. Standardization is out of the question; in the agrarian marketplace, quality varies from product to product, making each one somewhat unique and different from the others. Individuals in the marketplace, then, negotiate the price of each item according to its individual merits. It's a way of life for these societies, but the negotiating skill is tremendously important outside the marketplace, too. It's little wonder why our professional negotiators did such a poor job in dealing with the Iranian government during and after the hostage crisis. After all, the most important political and social institutions in Iran are the bazaars, where negotiations are the nucleus of activities.

As such, the purpose of this book is not to instruct you in the skill of conflict resolution, or "win-win" negotiating. *How to Outnegotiate Anyone* focuses on the type of negotiating we call "bargaining." Certainly, win-win negotiating is a valuable tool to resolving conflicts inside your company, your marriage, your community or your nation, but I would never recommend taking a "win-win" negotiating book onto a car lot or into a middle eastern bazaar. Chances are, they would take you to the proverbial cleaners if you did! There are a number of similarities between win-win and bargaining in the approach one takes to the negotiation process; being patient, knowing your needs, and maintaining a positive attitude are all essential characteristics of the effective negotiator in any situation, not just bargaining. However, one of the fundamental problems with using a win-win approach is that it generally requires a cooperative attitude from the other side. What happens if the other side doesn't elect to play along? What if their entire strategy is "win-lose?" In fact, this is precisely the attitude many people have when they are negotiating the purchase or sale of any item that has a significant impact on them in terms of cost or benefit.

In fact, mastering the art of bargaining is essential if you are going to successfully maneuver in those settings where bargaining is inevitably going to occur, such as buying a product or negotiating a contract. And it is my firm conviction that this process can be learned.

Bargaining effectively is relatively easy to do. You do not need any innate talent, special skills, or ability to argue effectively or to eloquently present positions in order to negotiate effectively. In fact, the bargaining process can be mastered by simply paying attention to certain fundamentals and applying them consistently.

The problem with the bargaining process is that there are many serious misconceptions about it. People tend to think that bargaining is a process of winning through intimidation, that it is a difficult process to master, or that a fair outcome or an improved relationship with the other side cannot be achieved. It is even argued from time to time that the bargaining process is fundamentally irrational and destructive. These arguments could not be further from the truth.

Bargaining does not have to be, and should not be, destructive to relationships. Indeed, if you are a successful negotiator, you have the ability to bargain effectively for price and terms while, at the same time, creating a positive relationship with the other side. The entire first chapter of this book shows why this is essential to your success and how it can be accomplished.

Bargaining is also not a fundamentally irrational process. It is only as irrational as we allow it to be. That is why this text pays particular attention to important decision-making skills, such as setting bottom lines, knowing when to deadlock, how to make an opening offer, and how to set and realize negotiating goals.

It is my hope that this book will enable you to master the bargaining process instead of being afraid of it.

Chapter One

The Power of Patience

If You Absolutely, Positively Have to Have Something Today, Buy It Tomorrow

Have you ever see that cartoon where some poor soul is crawling on his belly across the Sahara Desert calling out, "Water! Water!" Imagine you owned the only oasis for the next three hundred miles. Needless to say, this is not a person you would take seriously if he tried to negotiate the price of a bottle of Perrier. This is one person who is willing to pay full price.

Unfortunately, most buyers are like this fellow, willing to pay full-price because they urgently "need" the particular item. They get an impulse, and they act on it as if they were without a bottle of water in the desert. It's called "impulse buying," and sellers love it. Impulse buyers are the mother's milk of car lots and stereo stores.

The sad fact is, impulse buyers perpetually suffer from another buyer's disease called "buyer's remorse." Buyer's remorse usually happens when the buyer buys something he doesn't need. High pressure sales that lead to buyer's remorse have gotten so bad, many states now have "cool down" laws to protect car buyers from their own lack of patience.

Impatient negotiators are likely to reveal their bottom line early, make the opening offer unnecessarily, make poor opening offers, capitulate to intimidation or pressure tactics, make unnecessary concessions, and always pay too much—often without negotiating. Ironically, this attitude, which a seller can smell a mile away, usually has the effect of hardening the seller. Instead of causing negotiations to conclude quickly, the result is the seller hangs in there and becomes even more demanding.

Patient negotiators look confident, relaxed, and in control. They compare prices, determine if they really need a particular product and they always require justification for any concessions the sellers request. As such, they find it easier to control the process because they are not as anxious to close a deal. Car dealers, bank loan officers, sales and marketing personnel, building contractors, and others know this. As such, they generally do whatever they can to discover when or how you are likely to lose patience. Intimidation tactics, negotiating against your deadline, emotional outbursts, good guy-bad guy, and other assorted tactics are usually used with this in mind.

Be patient! Take your time! As an old trial lawyer friend of mine once said, "If you feel that you have to strike while the iron is hot, you are about to get your hands burned."

If You Insist On Having It Today, Know What You Want And Be Prepared to Pay For It

Know What You Want . . .
Recently, I was talking with a client who owns a string of fast food outlets in California. At the end of his fiscal year, he totaled up his sales and analyzed them. To nobody's surprise, one of the most successful tactics used by his employees was to ask the following question at the end of each order: "Would you like fries (or an apple turnover) with that order?" In over twenty percent of all cases, the answer was affirmative. The total increase in sales resulting from this question had a significant effect on his gross sales for the year.

This question is called the "add-on close," and it is responsible for buyers purchasing everything from service agreements to neckties, when they only initially intended to buy the base product (the car or the suit). Typical examples of the add-on close include the following:

- "Thank you for your order, Mr. Johnson. While you are at it, would you like to order an extra toner cartridge for your printer?"

- "You have just got a great deal on this suit, Mr. Robertson. Would you like to increase your savings by buying two suits instead of only one?"

- "You have just bought a beautiful car, Mr. Reilly. If you act quickly, I can give you a great deal on a service agreement for this automobile. How about it?"

Everyone knows you should never go shopping for groceries without bringing a list. Otherwise, you will come home with a month's supply of things you don't need, instead of what you really do need. Buying a car, a computer, or a house is no different from buying groceries. Know what you want before you buy. Then bring a list and stick to it.

The add-on close isn't the only way sellers induce us to buy more than we intended.[1] But it is the most common, and experience tells us it is the most effective.

. . . and Be Prepared To Pay For It.

Those who can't pay, don't play.

Five years ago, one of my employees had her eye on a beautiful Persian cat her neighbor was selling. Every day she offered the owner a price for the cat that was too low, and every day the owner turned her down. Finally, the owner sold the cat to another buyer for full-price. My secretary talks about that cat to this day. She has never seen another one just like it. Of course, had she to do it all over again, she would have paid whatever she had to get the cat. But this is hindsight.

To put it bluntly, if you absolutely, positively have to have something, you better be able to afford it. This is not to say you shouldn't try to negotiate price. However, if the product is not mass produced and the price is not nego-

---

[1] Playing Muzak in a grocery store, putting candy within a child's reach at a check-out stand, and offering free samples are the other ways that sellers cause people to purchase more than they intended.

tiable, and if you really want it, you had better pay before the opportunity is lost.

Why You Should Never Disclose Your Deadline

A friend of mine went on a business trip to Japan to negotiate a distribution agreement with a large Japanese electronics company. After he arrived in Tokyo, he was asked by his Japanese host when he would be returning to the United States. "We need to know so we can arrange to drive you back to the airport," he said. My friend replied he had to leave on Friday, so he could be back in the office the following Monday for a court appearance.

For the next five days, his Japanese hosts gave him tours of the company plant, long lunches, formal presentations, and speeches, everything except what he went to Japan for—to negotiate a deal. Finally, Friday morning, only five hours before his flight, negotiations began slowly.

Needless to say, he was under intense pressure to make concessions. Only then did the truth dawn on him. Because negotiations had been delayed until the last moment, he was put at a tremendous disadvantage. Imagine his client's surprise when he discovered that after sending his lawyer to the most expensive city in the world—at $300 an hour plus expenses—the most he was able to accomplish was some late night drinking and a golf game!

Remember: *The weakest party is the one that is negotiating against its own deadline,* while the other side is negotiating far in advance of its own.

Never disclose your deadline when you can avoid it. This information should be preserved at all costs. Too often, we either answer the wrong question (such as, "When do you need it?") or we volunteer the information ourselves. It is bad enough we are already under significant pressure when we negotiate against our deadlines. The real tragedy is that when the other side knows this, they tend to become tougher negotiators to deal with. This is a sure-fire formula for disaster.

Sales and marketing departments are usually under

pressure to increase sales as the company's quarter end nears.[2] There is no reason for management to broadcast this fact, as they do in the computer industry. Similarly, information about hotel check-out times, vacation plans, flight arrangements, project schedules, and so on, should all be zealously guarded if they will have an impact on negotiations.

Office staff should be given information about negotiating deadlines on a "need to know" basis only. The easiest way for your adversaries to gather information about your deadline is for them to simply ask a low-level staff member, such as a secretary or receptionist.

People who must know about your deadlines, such as an appointment secretary, should be informed of the importance of keeping this information confidential. It is a good idea to sit down with your staff on a regular basis and discuss the impact this information can have on the company's negotiations, in order to encourage discretion. If people in your office are not sure what information is important and what information isn't, then the old adage should apply: "Discretion is the better part of valor."

What to do When You Have Already Disclosed Your Deadline

Imagine that your boss came into your office with a project and said: "We need to have this contract negotiated by next Thursday. I just called the other side and advised them that we have an impending deadline and that this contract has to be completed pronto. Now go out and try to get a good deal. You are always getting taken by these guys!"

Recently, a procurement officer for the United States Army told me about just such a problem. Three weeks before the Army was set to move into a new building, it was discovered that no phone lines had been installed, while

---

[2] I doubt that there is a purchasing department in the country that doesn't know that computer companies offer big discounts on the sale of their products if (a) the end of the quarter or fiscal year is nearing; and (b) their stock is publicly traded. The reason for these large discounts is that as these companies approach the end of their fiscal quarter, they pressure their sales staff to generate cash flow in order to support the price of their company stock.

the interior walls of the building were going to be installed in only a matter of days. The commanding officer called the only contractor in the entire state who was free to do the job and advised him that the lines had to be installed in five days. Needless to say, the contractor increased his price by an outrageous amount. What could the procurement officer do? Didn't the contractor have her over a barrel? Perhaps. Perhaps not.

Most deadlines are negotiable

Most deadlines are merely inspirational. They are set up for no other reason than to motivate people to meet that deadline. Any project manager will tell you that if you ask someone to complete a very specific task within a short period of time, it is more likely to be completed than if it is spread over a greater period of time and is more general in its description. In fact, the smaller the task and the shorter the deadline, the greater the likelihood the task will be done well and on time. A deadline, therefore, is an important motivational tool in any organization, but it is not a good reason to get gouged in negotiations. Occasionally, there are legitimate reasons for a deadline to exist, but you should never try to negotiate against a deadline without first determining if better alternatives are not available. A good way to determine this is to follow the five-step process below.

1. *Ask Yourself: Who set the deadline?* Deadlines do not fall out of the sky. Nor are they the result of the natural laws of physics. Deadlines are set by people who are usually very close to us, often our immediate superiors. As such, if we approach the issue correctly, we may be able to change the deadline rather than negotiate against it. And, before you can negotiate the deadline, you need to know who has the authority to change it.

2. *What was the reason for setting the deadline?* Why was this deadline created in the first place? In other words, what underlying needs does this deadline address? Sometimes the needs are compelling, such as meeting a construction schedule, a

tax deadline, etc. On most occasions, however, there is a motivational reason for the deadline and nothing more. If the consequences of failing to meet the deadline are drastic, then your willingness to grin and bear it while you are getting gouged will probably be fairly high.

3. *Educate 'em.* Approach the person who set the deadline and explain the impact it is having on your ability to negotiate. *Be careful to be especially polite and diplomatic about it.* If you make the other person defensive, he will usually marry the deadline in order to save face and refuse to change it. Instead of using accusatory language—"Don't you know what you have done to my bargaining position?"—use an "us versus them" approach—"I thought you should know what they are trying to do to us in the face of our deadline. I wanted to see if there was something that we could do together to deal with this person."

4. *Discuss Your Bottom Line.* The best way to determine if it is feasible to set back the deadline is to ask the following question: "What is the cost of changing the deadline as opposed to the cost of negotiating against it?" If the cost of changing the deadline is less than the cost of getting gouged, as it usually is, then you have an excellent argument for moving back the deadline. On the other hand, if it is more costly to change the deadline, then at least you have made a rational decision to get gouged.

5. *And when all else fails . . .* If you must negotiate against a deadline, downplay its importance when you are negotiating with the other side. Don't allow the fact that you are under the pressure of the deadline to become the focus of negotiations. Try to keep the focus of the negotiations on the inherent validity of the deal itself.

If the other side is taking advantage of the situation, let them know that you are cognizant of the fact that you are being "taken." It is also a good idea to keep the focus of negotiations on the fact that they cannot provide a reasonable, objective, justification for their position.

Why Car Dealers Will Never Let You Off the Lot Alive

Several years ago, I visited a client who had been selling cars in California for over 15 years. One Saturday afternoon, as he was monitoring a number of different negotiations that were going on, he pointed out a middle-aged couple that had been negotiating for a car for over three hours. From my perspective, it looked as if the deal was going to fall apart. The parties were relatively far apart on price and terms and little progress was being made, or so I thought.

"Relax," the dealer said. "The longer they negotiate, the harder it is for them to walk away." In fact, the deal was closed 30 minutes later. Two days later, in a meeting at my office, the dealer explained. "For most people, negotiating is like a root canal. It doesn't matter what you are negotiating about. People hate to negotiate. It's that simple. The longer they negotiate, the more likely they will make those hard concessions that they thought they would never make when they first walked in the door. And besides, if they deadlock, what are they going to do? Go to another car lot and start the whole process over again from scratch?"

Benjamin Franklin once said that time is money. I would add that time is a lot more than just money. It is also energy, aggravation, work piling up at the office, a missed football game, or the lost opportunity to do something you really enjoy. Whatever it is to most of us, the more time we invest in negotiations, the less willing we are to walk away without getting something out of our investment. That's why car dealers never let you off the lot alive!

Chapter Two

The Power of a Positive Relationship

Lower Their Shield and
Get Their Sword on the Table

Car dealers know that buyers hate their guts. They talk about it in seminars. Nobody trusts dealers, nobody likes them, and nobody really wants to do business with them. I doubt that there is any other profession, except Congressmen and lawyers, that causes people to react at such a gut level. This makes selling cars a particularly difficult way to make a living.

Think back to the last time you walked onto a car lot. You probably saw a group of salesmen standing around in a circle talking. The moment you put your foot on the lot they all turned and looked at you at the same time. Suddenly, one of them peeled off from the group and began to move in on you at two o'clock, like a fighter jet breaking formation. At this point, there was probably only one thing going through your mind: "These bastards took me to the cleaners the last time that I was here, and they are going to do it again."

This is, in fact, the worst possible time for a car dealer to try to make a sale. You are rightly suspicious of everything he tells you and are looking for a reason to walk away. No matter what he says to you, you are inclined to disbelieve it; if he says it's a beautiful day, you check to see if it is raining.

A good car dealer always starts off by backing off and

giving the buyer space. If he comes on too fast or too hard, he will probably see his buyer turn tail and run. Instead, if he knows what he is doing, he will start by using a light, non-threatening touch. He will introduce himself and usually tell you something about himself. This personal touch shows he is a human being, just like you, and not a demon from the eighth circle of hell. He will then ask you non-threatening questions in order to determine just what kind of a buyer you are and what type of automobile you are interested in buying. He will tell you to relax and take your time. "You just find the car you want," he'll say, "and I'll make you a deal that will knock your socks off." After you have zeroed in on a specific model and make of car, he will then compliment you on your choice and ask you if you would like to take it for a test drive, the buyer's ultimate bonding experience.

The test drive is, of course, for the benefit of the seller, not the buyer. During the test drive, you begin to visualize yourself as the owner of the car. You also begin to notice certain things, like the new car's responsive suspension system! And by this time, you are beginning to think: "Gee, Bob isn't such a bad guy after all." You have now lowered your shield and are putting your sword on the table.

This car dealer obviously understands an important key to successful negotiating: It is easier to negotiate with friends than with enemies. People who like or trust us are more likely to cut us slack and give us concessions than people who don't like us or trust us. If you want to make enemies, don't make them until negotiations are over.

If They Don't Think a Deal Is Possible, It Isn't

There is a judge in Los Angeles County who has been trying divorce cases for as long as I can remember. He is a favorite among attorneys because of his amazing ability to settle difficult cases.

During a family law seminar he was conducting for divorce lawyers, I asked him what his secret was to making these settlements. He told me a story about the worst divorce case he had ever handled. This was the divorce to end all divorces. No two people could ever have hated each other more than these people did. To prove it, they fought over who got custody of the two children, what the support should be, what visitation should be, who got the assets, who paid the debts, who got the house, who got the family pets, where the kids would be educated, who got what cars, and so on. They fought over anything and everything.

Finally, the case was scheduled for a settlement conference. The judge told me that when he met with opposing counsels and their clients, he lied to them about their case. He said, "I've seen worse." (He hadn't.) Then he fabricated a story about this other case, giving detail by bloody detail. Finally, the judge surprised the parties by announcing that even that case—the proverbial War of the Roses—settled. He concluded by telling the husband and wife, in the presence of their lawyers, that he had never seen a case that couldn't be settled, and their case was certainly no exception. By this time, the parties were starting to feel that perhaps their case wasn't that bad after all.

Get Them Engaged

The starting point for any successful negotiator is to get the other side engaged in the negotiation process. When they become engaged, and start to invest time and energy, they are less willing to just walk away and abandon the deal. There is a greater likelihood they will make concessions they thought they would never make when they first began negotiating.

My favorite car dealer is a fellow in California known as Cal Worthington. Cal is a master at getting his buyers initially engaged. He brags that he will do anything, *anything*, to sell a car. This includes wrestling with a tiger, riding a water buffalo, kissing a monkey, lying in the path of a walking elephant, and (my personal favorite) eating a bug. The implication is that if this guy will eat a bug to sell a car, he will certainly make monetary concessions! If you intend to negotiate successfully with the other side, you must communicate a sense of optimism about your ability to find a deal with them. This is why car dealers and other salespersons always try to instill a sense of optimism in their buyers, as well as in themselves. They want to get us engaged in the process so we will be unwilling to walk off the lot without a car.

Remember, if the other side believes a deal is possible, it probably is. If they don't believe a deal is possible, it probably isn't.

Nine Ways to Calm Them Down and Mellow Them Out

1. *Try not to look like you ate a lemon for breakfast.* Smile! At least occasionally. When we first walk into a room to negotiate we are usually on guard and more than a little tense. This causes us to look negative, even when we are not, and more than a little defensive. It also makes us look a little unsure of ourselves. Conversely, if you are pleasant and positive, you will appear confident and will have an easier time taking control of the situation. Try to lighten up the atmosphere a little. Nothing is more fruitless than using positive language while looking like you just heard your favorite relative was hit by a train. A smile is the cheapest concession you can make and the best way of lowering the other side's shield.

2. *Use their first name.* Americans are, by nature, an informal people. With the possible exception of Richard Nixon and British royalty, people like to be called by their first names. If you act in a formal manner when you negotiate, you will tend to have arm's-length negotiations. The better way is to try to build as many personal bridges with the other side as you can. The more you can get the other side to treat you as a friend, rather than an adversary, the easier you will find it to get concessions from them.

3. *Ease into negotiations.* Don't launch right in. Relax. Take your time. Engage in small talk. Offer them coffee. Discuss anything that sets a personal tone to the negotiations. Of course, it helps if you know

something personal about the other side, like hobbies, sporting interests, children, to use in this opening conversation. Your goal is to break the ice sufficiently to help the other side relax and develop some type of contact with you beyond a formal business relationship.

4. *Be optimistic, or at least act like you are.* A friend of mine purchased a home in Palo Alto, California, three years ago. Since it was a depressed real estate market and because my friend was in no hurry to buy, his opening offer was significantly less than what the seller expected to receive. As a result, the negotiations continued for several weeks. Eventually, my friend received an offer that was close, but not close enough, to what he could afford. He sensed that it was a last and final offer and that the deal was in some jeopardy. Before he responded, however, he made a point of telling the seller's broker that the parties were "very close" and that he was "very, very optimistic that a deal would be done." He added that it would take him a few days to study the offer but on the face of it, it looked very positive.

The last-minute expression of optimism is one of my favorite closing tactics. It is particularly effective if the other side is under some pressure to close. When you let the other side know that you are very optimistic a deal will be made, it has the effect of causing them to visualize, even begin to plan for, the successful sale of their home. As a result, they are more likely to begin making plans to move and perhaps put an offer on another house. Even if it becomes apparent that they will have to make additional concessions in order to close, they will find it harder to walk away from negotiations.

Similarly, an optimistic attitude at the early stages of negotiations helps you get the other side engaged, making you look confident and in control of the process. Once the other side becomes engaged in the process, the likelihood that they will

continue to make concessions is high and becomes
even higher as the process continues.

5. *Use confidence building gestures (CBG's).* Former
Secretary of State Baker's main complaint against
the Israelis, Palestinians, and Arabs at the Madrid
Round of the Middle East peace negotiations was
not that the parties were unwilling to make early
concessions—nobody could rationally expect concessions to be easily made by either Arabs or Israelis in such difficult negotiations—but rather
that neither side was willing to use confidence
building gestures at the outset of negotiations. Instead, they accused each other of being "terrorists"
and of not negotiating in good faith. The result was
that opportunities for negotiating were being lost
even before negotiations got underway.

A confidence building gesture is any gesture you
can make that increases the other side's confidence
in the negotiating process. Remember, confidence
building gestures are just that—*gestures*. They are
not concessions. They are usually the easiest and
cheapest way to get the other side interested in the
negotiation process and the concession-making
that will be required from both sides. These gestures can include:

- expressing your intention to negotiate in good
  faith

- discussing the importance of achieving a deal
  that is fair for both sides

- acknowledging legitimate concerns the other
  side has

- showing an interest in the concerns and fears
  the other side has

- indicating a willingness to work hard to
  achieve an agreement satisfactory to both
  sides

6. *Search for common ground before you discuss your
differences.* A study of actual negotiations shows

that effective negotiators give as much as three times the attention to common ground issues than do average negotiators.[3] According to the report, skilled negotiators spend an average of 38 percent of the negotiating time discussing areas of anticipated agreement or common ground. Average negotiators, on the other hand, only spend an average of 11 percent of the negotiations making comments about anticipated agreement or common ground.

When you focus on common ground, you help to reinforce the other side's impression that a deal that will benefit *both* sides is possible. This makes it more likely that they will be willing to take the risk of offering concessions to you in order to achieve a deal.

The common ground that you share with the other side can include:

- *Common interests:* a deadline that is known to both sides that also affects both parties, a client that both parties need to please, a project that both parties need to complete

- *Common values:* shared religious beliefs, shared political convictions, or shared social perspectives

- *Common problems:* the cost of the dispute, such as attorney's fees, both sides' loss of face in the workplace, or the loss of control of the solution (i.e., If we don't solve this problem ourselves, someone else may solve it for us)

- *Anticipated agreement:* certain issues you believe are likely to be easily resolved, called to the other side's attention early and repeatedly to increase their belief that the other issues can be resolved as well

7. *State their position better than they can, even if you disagree.* Most negotiators believe that the best

---

[3] *Behavior of Successful Negotiators*, Huthwaite Research Group Report, 1976, 1992.

way to deal with the other side is to pay little or no attention to their strong points and even to belittle legitimate arguments they may have. In fact, this is a particularly destructive way to negotiate. By refusing to acknowledge valid points in their favor, you only create a more distrustful atmosphere for negotiating.[4] The best negotiators do just the opposite. If you can state the other side's position better than they can, while still indicating that you disagree, you will accomplish two things:

First, you will be better able to see the problem as they see it. This enables you to address their real concerns, not the ones you may think they have. Second, you will be better able to convince them of your position. The other side will be more likely to listen to your viewpoint when they believe you understand their position, too.

Remember, acknowledging the other side's viewpoint does not mean you accept it as being valid, but it does indicate that you have heard and understood what the other side had to say on that point.

8. *Promote privacy.* Jim is upset with Dan and intends to do something about it. Dan refuses to complete his work on a project until the very last moment when he dumps it on Jim's desk. Jim's plans for the weekend are always ruined because of Dan's irresponsibility. Furthermore, Jim is given almost no lead time to complete his work. The upshot of it all is that the quality of Jim's work is not what it should be because of the time pressures caused by Dan's procrastination. Jim ends up getting the blame for the resulting shoddy work when the problem should be laid at Dan's doorstep.

---

[4] Sometimes we do this without even realizing it. Researchers at the Stanford Center on Conflict and Negotiation have shown that people tend to devalue the worth of the concessions that are being offered to them by the other side, while simultaneously overvaluing the worth of their own concessions. The "Reactive Devaluation" Barrier to Conflict Resolution, Stanford Center on Conflict and Negotiation Working Paper Series, December 1988, Constance A. Stillinger, Michael Epelbaum, Dacher Keltner and Lee Ross.

Dan regards Jim as a "whiner" who is afraid of hard work and is always looking to blame others for his own laziness. Dan works weekends regularly and has always finished his projects on time, even though he is frequently under the same time pressures as Jim.

Both Jim and Dan have complained openly to their colleagues about the other. As the dispute is publicized throughout the workplace, people begin to gossip and there is open speculation as to who will "win" the fight that is underway. Even worse, some people begin to choose sides.

At this point, the opportunities for a successful negotiation between Dan and Jim have been severely damaged. People tend to play to the gallery when they negotiate. If they think they will "look like a wimp" to their friends and colleagues by making a particular deal, they are less likely to do so even if they firmly believe that the deal is a good one.

In short, the more public negotiations are, the greater the likelihood of a deadlock. If you have to resolve a particular problem with someone, try to do it in a setting that is away from prying eyes and open ears. Try to promote privacy with the other side whenever possible.

- Resolve your disputes privately and away from the eyes and ears of others. Find a quiet setting, such as a conference room, office, or restaurant, out of the sight and hearing of third parties.

- Don't talk about your negotiations with people who are not involved.

- Try to elicit an agreement from the other side about keeping the negotiations and their results confidential.

- Try to resolve your problems quickly, before they become the subject of public speculation and discussion.

9. *Help them to save face.* Americans are highly con-

scious of saving face, and when we lose it, we do something uniquely American. We retaliate. If the other side is in this position, they are more difficult to deal with. Here's how to help adversaries save face:

- *Never point out that they have backed off a position if you don't have to.* Using words such as, "you really haven't backed down, circumstances have changed," can be the deciding factor in whether the other side makes a painful concession or not.

- *Try to give them a way out of their dilemma.* Professor William Ury, of Harvard University, likes to say: "Give the other side a golden bridge to retreat across."[5] During the Cuban Missile Crisis, Kennedy put a blockade around Cuba in order to prevent any Soviet ships from entering Cuban waters. Khrushchev vowed to break this blockade. Because neither side could back down without suffering public humiliation, the prospects for nuclear war between the two superpowers was seen as being almost inevitable. Then John Kennedy offered to pull American missiles out of Turkey if Khrushchev would pull his missiles out of Cuba. This appearance of a quid pro quo exchange of concessions was the fig leaf that allowed the Soviet Union to back down from its previously declared position. A nuclear war was averted.

- *Look for ways to help them sell the deal to others.* This is especially true if they depend on approval from a boss, a client, a colleague, or a spouse.

The "Banana Pellet" Theory of Negotiating

During the early stages of the space program, NASA sent

---

[5] *Getting Past No*, Houghton Mifflin, 1992, William Ury.

chimpanzees into outer space before it sent astronauts. During the flight, they used banana pellets as an incentive to get the chimps to perform the tasks they needed accomplished while they were in orbit. If the chimp flipped a switch when it was supposed to, a banana pellet was dispensed into a cup for the chimp to eat. Needless to say, it rarely took long for the chimp to learn what to do whenever a reward was offered for doing it.[6]

Let the other side know you will respond positively if they can rationally justify their position. People are ultimately rational when they negotiate. They will do whatever works. If you give concessions to buy people off of bad behavior, you will inevitably get more bad behavior. Conversely, if you want the other side to engage in rational behavior, you should always reward them with concessions when they behave rationally. Let them know that if they can provide a reasonable justification for their position, you will respond positively. Then when they do act rationally, show movement. Acknowledge their points. Give concessions. Make compromises. Within a short period of time, they will understand what works and what doesn't, and they will invariably act accordingly.

Nobody Likes to Look Stupid for a Prolonged Period of Time

Ask George Steinbrenner!

At first, being bloody-minded at the table can be fun. If nothing is accomplished by it quickly, however, it tends to get tiresome for the person who is doing it.

Always provide justification for every position you take in any negotiation and insist the other side does the same. If the other side takes an irrational position, simply focus on the irrationality of their position. Let them know that if they can provide a rational justification, you will respond

---

[6] This can work in unexpected ways. During one phase of the program, they were using chimpanzees to test ejection seats. When they strapped one chimp into the seat, he became nervous and excitable. One of the engineers gave him a banana to calm him down. After he relaxed, they ejected him. Several weeks later he was strapped into the seat for another test. The chimp began to panic. The same engineer offered the chimp another banana. Instead of taking the banana, this time the chimp went berserk.

positively. But always keep the focus on the lack of any underlying rationale for their position. By doing so, you keep
the ball firmly in their side of the court. This not only tends
to give you momentum and control, but it also tests their
patience with their own position. And nobody likes to look
stupid, at least not for long.

Chapter Three

Deadlocking

The "I'll See You In Hell" Syndrome

For most of the 1980s, Eastern Airlines and the mechanics union fought a bitter battle that eventually bankrupted the company and cost the employees their jobs. In retrospect, it is easy to say there should have been some way to have reached an agreement, one that could have left both the company and its employees better off. Almost any agreement would have been better than what they ended up with: a bankrupt company and an unemployed work force. What was so important to each side that they were willing to risk the life of the company and the jobs of the workers?

The question is almost academic. Unless fundamental issues such as worker safety (life being more important than a job) or freedom of speech were at risk, hardly any demand would have justified the death of a company and the resulting unemployment of its workers.[7] Yet that is precisely what happened. And the Eastern Airlines- Mechanics Union negotiation is hardly the rare exception to the rule. Ask any divorce lawyer. People derive, at least in

---

[7] Three years after the strike ended, the Eastern Airlines deadlock was even having ramifications in the union's dealings with other carriers. The demise of Eastern Airlines, and the resulting unemployment of its members, left District 100 of the International Association of Machinists and Aerospace Workers far behind in paying its own debts, including its share of the bill owed to arbitrators who were hearing disputes between the union and other airline carriers. As a result, the arbitrators refused to hold additional hearings until the union squared its accounts. This gave the other airlines increased clout, since they could give the union two alternatives: either to accept their contract proposal or go to arbitration. Since the union wouldn't be able to go to arbitration, it would be put, as it were, on the horns of a dilemma. (Source: *Aviation Week and Space Technology*, April 20, 1992, page 15.)

the short run, a certain satisfaction from "seeing us in Hell" that almost transcends the satisfaction they would get in obtaining a successful deal.

Most deadlocks tend to occur within the zone of agreement. This is to say that both parties to the negotiation would have been better off if either of them had accepted the last offer the other side made than if they had deadlocked, so they deadlocked anyway.

Most deadlocks are caused by ego. Never underestimate the willingness of the other side to cut off their nose to spite their face, if they can cut off yours as well. Challenging the other side, engaging in brinkmanship or arguing that a deadlock will hurt them more than it will hurt you, are usually tactics that result in retaliation and the conflict's escalation. In Eastern Airlines' case, this strategy brinkmanship, retaliation, and escalation continued over a decade. By the time the parties entered into the last phase of their dispute, neither was particularly interested in rational negotiations. Each side regarded the dispute as a war that could only be won or lost unconditionally. In the end, the only winners were the other airlines and, of course, the lawyers.

Why Dwelling On Deadlocked Issues Is Incredibly Stupid (And Why Everybody Does It)

A favorite old story of mine is the one about the guy who kept hitting himself on the head with a hammer. "Why are you doing that?" asked an onlooker. "Because it feels so good when I stop," he replied.

Dwelling on deadlocked issues is no different. It is a useless exercise in futility. The longer you dwell on deadlocked issues, the more likely you will deadlock. Both sides disengage each other from the process, create less incentives for making concessions, and infuse a general sense of pessimism into negotiations.

When you get to a deadlocked issue, move on. Find as many other areas of agreement as you can. Then return to the deadlocked issue later. Try to determine if the deadlock is being caused by the parties' egos or by some substantive difference in opinion. If the differences are mainly ego, a cool down period may be the best solution. If the deadlock is the result of substantive differences, consider brainstorming with others in order to find creative solutions to the problems causing the deadlock. By moving off deadlocked issues you:

- maintain your own patience when the other side may lose theirs

- have a better opportunity to keep the other side engaged

- give the other side an opportunity to "cool down" and reconsider their position

- give yourself time to consider ways to break the deadlock

- prevent deadlock from occurring prematurely or unnecessarily

- lessen the chances of egos getting involved

Everything *Isn't* Negotiable

There is a time to deadlock. As John Wayne once said, "Sometimes a man has gotta do what a man has gotta do." One of the common myths that is perpetuated about negotiation is that "everything is negotiable". In fact, everything *is not* negotiable . . . and if it is, it probably shouldn't be. Negotiation involves compromise, and certain things in life simply cannot be compromised. They have to be faced squarely and acknowledged for what they are.

Let's start with values. If someone is willing to compromise his values, he is probably not worth much respect. The principles that make us what we are both as individuals and as a civilized society cannot simply be bargained away or regarded as expendable. For some of us, these principles are based on religious convictions; for others, they are simply ideals worth fighting, even dying, for. When demonstrators in Birmingham, Atlanta, or in a hundred other cities in this country sat in at the white sections of lunch counters, rather than move to the "colored" sections of the restaurant, they demonstrated openly that they were not interested in bargaining over, and compromising away, their constitutional rights. These issues were simply non-negotiable. Thousands went to jail, suffered physical abuse, and even died just to prove the point.

In a similar vein, the fundamental awareness of the non-negotiability of moral issues is what permeates the public's dissatisfaction with plea bargaining in certain criminal cases. When I was studying criminal procedure in law school, my professor told me a short story that drives this home. He swears this story is true:

After feverishly bargaining with the district attorney, a defense attorney returned to his client and proudly told him of the great deal he struck, a misdemeanor conviction with no jail time. After 30 minutes passed, he returned with startling news. The defendant refused to agree. There was no deal. The D.A. was angry, the judge was incredulous, and the defense attorney was embarrassed. The defense attorney was advised to discuss the matter again with his client. Didn't he know what a sweet deal this was? Didn't he know he could go to prison if he was convicted? The defense attorney went back to his client to try to persuade him to see reason. His client screamed back in fury, "But I'm innocent!" The case went to trial and it took the jury only one hour to return a verdict of not guilty.

If something isn't negotiable, for heaven's sake, don't negotiate! And don't be tricked into believing that there is a difference between negotiations and "discussions." You will only be pressured to make compromises you cannot or should not make. And don't think you will be able to outlast the other side. Once negotiations are underway, the understanding is implicit that you should be making compromises if you are to be seen as acting in good faith. Letting the other side know that you are non-negotiable before negotiations get underway usually doesn't work either. They will think you are simply posturing. The pressure for you to break down and compromise will become enormous. Once the other side realizes you are serious and you will not be making compromises on the non-negotiable issues, they will become even angrier than they would have been had you simply nixed the idea of compromise at the outset.

When to Deadlock and When Not To

The most powerful negotiator is the one who knows when to walk away without looking back. These negotiators usually control the negotiating process. They are more likely to strike better deals. Most importantly, they tend to have a high level of self-confidence of which the other side becomes aware early in the negotiating process. A ripple effect then occurs that works to their benefit throughout the remainder of the negotiating session. Because the other side respects them, they are less likely to play games or use pressure tactics to get what they want. This makes for a more positive, rational atmosphere for the parties to work in. This then creates more opportunities for a positive ongoing working relationship after negotiations are concluded, and it leads to easier subsequent negotiations as well. If you know when to deadlock and when not to deadlock you will:

- be less likely to act irrationally at the table
- be less likely to cut bad deals
- appear confident and in control
- be less susceptible to pressure tactics
- be less likely to make decisions based on ego

Before you begin to negotiate, you should go through the following mental process:

First, visualize deadlock. Visualize what your situation will be if negotiations result in deadlock. The benefit of this visualization process is that it forces you to confront the reality of a deadlock before it occurs, not after. If, for example, you are about to negotiate the purchase of a Ford Taurus, imagine that the dealership will not sell you that Ford Taurus for a million dollars in cash. In other words, there is no way you are going to be able to successfully negotiate the purchase of that automobile.

Second, determine what alternatives are available to you. Recently, I was teaching a seminar at the University of California. A young man approached me who was about to interview with several high tech companies in Southern California and a number of other companies on the East Coast. When I asked him which companies he was going to interview first, he replied, "The ones in Silicon Valley, of course." "Why?" I asked. "Because I grew up in this area," he said. "Besides," he continued, "I think I would enjoy living here more anyway. The East Coast is an area that I rarely travel to. I don't know anyone over there and I'm not sure I would like the weather," he said. So I asked why he was even considering the companies on the East Coast. He smiled. "Obviously, if they make me a better offer, I'll consider it," he said. "Especially if it is an offer that I can't refuse." "So, bearing in mind that your first choice is to work in California, where are you going to interview first?" I asked. "California," he replied. "Wrong. Go to the East Coast first," I told him. "Get the best offer you can and take it back to California with you. Now you will know when to deadlock in California and when not to."

The problem with this young man's approach is that if he were to start off interviewing with the companies he was most interested in, he would have no criteria for judging what a good outcome for him would be. By determining his alternatives to negotiating first, he not only creates some objective standard for determining what a good deal is, but he also increases his confidence level by having the information. He becomes a more powerful negotiator.

Now, determine the best alternative you have to negotiating. Let's go back to the car lot. We have already visualized a deadlock occurring. Now, ask yourself, "Assuming that I am unable to successfully negotiate the purchase of this Taurus from this particular dealership, what are the very best alternatives I have to these negotiations?" At this juncture, they may be numerous. They could include:

- simply going to another dealership and starting over, a pretty good alternative when you consider that the only cost is your time and effort

- buying a different model or brand of car, something you should always consider in any case

- fixing up your existing automobile and driving it for another 40,000 miles
- using public transport
- sharing rides with someone from the office
- doing nothing (i.e. not buying a new car after all)

The idea is to pick the very best alternative you have to negotiating in the event of a deadlock.[8] Anytime the other side makes you an offer that is better than this "best alternative", it is an offer you should not ultimately turn down. Conversely, anytime you receive an offer that is not as good as your "best alternative," it is an offer you can turn down with a high degree of confidence. After all, by deadlocking, you are still left better off than if you had accepted the last offer that had been made to you by the other side. You will not only be able to say "no" to the other side with the confidence of a powerful negotiator, but you will also be able to explain *why* you are saying no in a rational and convincing manner.

What if you have no alternatives to negotiating? It is rare that a negotiator has no alternatives to a negotiated outcome besides deadlocking, which is itself an alternative. The alternatives open to you may not be very satisfactory, but they are there nonetheless and will help you to properly define your situation.

Recently, the purchasing agent for a corporate client of mine called me to discuss a dilemma he faced. His company manufactured computers. They preferred to use an "optical" instead of a mechanical mouse for their computers.[9] There is only one company in the world that manufactures the optical mouse and they were temporarily backlogged with orders. Unfortunately, he needed several

---

[8] Roger Fisher and William Ury of Harvard University refer to this as your "BATNA" (best alternative to a negotiated agreement). *Getting to Yes*, Houghton Mifflin, 1981, Roger Fisher and William Ury.

[9] A mechanical mouse uses a roller ball to move around. An optical mouse, on the other hand, has no moving parts. It shines a light on a special mirrored pad which reflects that light back to the mouse, in order to determine how far or fast you have moved the mouse.

thousand optical mice immediately. What were his alternatives and what was their cost? For example, what would happen if he put off the purchase of the mice? Would a customer account be lost? What would the ultimate cost of that lost account be? Would a project be delayed? What would be the cost of that delay? Furthermore, what would be the implications of switching to a mechanical mouse? In other words, just how important is it to purchase an optical mouse for these computers? Why is the company married to the optical mouse in the first place? How much more expensive than a mechanical mouse is an optical mouse? Is the optical mouse more or less reliable? What if he purchased mechanical mice now and replaced them with optical mice later? Of course, this double expenditure is costly, but is it more or less costly than waiting for the optical mice to become available? What if he purchased no mice at all? Is the mouse necessary to operate the software that is going to be used?

The benefits that come from this kind of pre-negotiation analysis are readily apparent. You begin to learn just how much you really "need" something. This tells you how much you should be prepared to pay for it. This is one reason why corporate purchasing departments should regularly review their sole-source vendor accounts. In particular, they should regularly determine if there is any new competition in the marketplace and, more importantly, whether the need for the product is still as great as was initially determined. If the need is great and there is no competition, be prepared to pay full price. Conversely, if the need is less or if new competition exists, you are in a better position to negotiate.

Finally, if you truly have no alternatives to negotiating with the other side, then you are a very weak negotiator indeed. In this situation, the very worst thing that you can do is to engage in brinkmanship and start bluffing about your bottom line.

"This is my last and final offer"

An old friend of mine from college loves to play poker. Although I wouldn't call him a professional gambler, he is the closest thing to one I have ever met. One weekend, he joined me for a friendly game of low stakes poker at a colleague's house on a late Friday night. Before the evening was over, he was sitting at one end of the table with all of the chips while the rest of us were broke, or very close to it. On the way home, I asked him what his secret was. "It's not how I was playing so much as it was how the rest of you were playing," he said. "You guys bluff too much! You are always bluffing." The problem is that most bluffs get called. This leads to disaster. The best poker players play straight statistical poker for most of the evening until the perfect situation presents itself. Then they run their bluff. Because they have only been challenging the other players when they have strong hands, the other players have gotten into the habit of believing them whenever they up the ante.

In negotiating, the best negotiators *never* bluff. As in poker, this is because almost all bluffs get called. And the more you bluff unsuccessfully, the greater the likelihood the other side will continue calling your bluff.

The words, "This is my last and final offer," constitute the most common bluff used in negotiations by tactical negotiators. The truth is that people rarely mean it when they use this threat. Almost always they are engaging in a game of "chicken" or brinkmanship. The interesting thing is that "last and final offers" are not only the most common bluff, but they are also the most commonly called bluff. They rarely work because people rarely believe we mean it when we say we have stopped negotiating. In fact, the only thing that last and final offers really do is make the other side curious as to whether we really mean what we say or if we are just posturing. As with excessive bluffing in the game of poker, this leads to disaster. If you are truly making your last and final offer, be prepared to offer a detailed explanation as to why you cannot make any further concessions than you already have.

Similarly, when confronted with a "last and final offer" from the other side, don't panic. Don't focus so much on their "unalterable" position. Probe their reasons for making the offer final and attempt to determine what their actual needs are. It may also be a good idea to give them an opportunity to cool down and reconsider their position. The main thing is not to lose patience.

Chapter Four

Offers And Counter-Offers

Recently, at a seminar I was giving in Seattle, Washington, a real estate broker told me about a sale that took her less than 15 minutes to close. A newly married couple walked through a home that had just been put on the market. The market was very slow and it was a safe bet that the sellers would be very negotiable when it came to discussing price and terms. Within five minutes of entering the home, the couple asked the broker what the asking price for the house was. The broker responded by saying that the sellers were asking for $185,000. She was just about to add that she thought the sellers would be willing to come down from that price when the buyers cut her off: "Wow!," they replied, "That's a lot less than we expected to pay for a house like this!" Needless to say, the seller underwent an immediate change in attitude. Instead of offering any significant concessions in price, the seller only made very modest concessions in price and refused to negotiate further. The deal closed on essentially the seller's terms.

The Opening Offer: Blow It And You're Dead

The very worst mistake any negotiator can make is blowing the opening offer. It is difficult, if not impossible, to recover from a blown opening offer. The reason is that the opening offer tends to set the other side's expectations as to what will happen during the balance of the negotiation session. If the other side's expectations are set unnecessarily high, you will have to prepare for them to be seriously disappointed when reality presents itself. If the opening offer sets the others side's expectations unnecessarily low, deadlock at the outset of negotiations can occur or, at the very least, tensions can arise and harden their position later on. Finally, as with the young couple who were buying their first home, a blown opening offer can lock us into a bad position early and make it difficult for us to escape from that position.

Use your brain before you open your mouth

The greatest single mistake you can make at the beginning stages of negotiations is simply not thinking carefully about your opening offer before you open your mouth. Resist the temptation to "get down to brass tacks" too early. Try to gather some information from the other side before you define your position. Ask yourself the following questions:

- What is it that the other side is trying to accomplish by negotiating?
- What is their perception of value?
- Do they appear to be flexible or inflexible?
- What do I need to know about the other side's position or perceptions before I begin to negotiate?

Remember, your opening offer has a direct impact on how negotiations proceed, whether you are able to keep the other side engaged in the process, and what their attitudes are toward negotiations as well as toward you. In short, opening offers are the first indication the other side receives from you as to how negotiations are going to proceed. Be patient and move carefully.

Wrong-Way Boulware's Fatal Mistake

Two years ago, I was teaching a seminar to members of the Army Corps of Engineers. At the end of a two-day class, one of the attendees, who had said nothing during the entire presentation, finally spoke up. "This information is fine," he said, "but frankly, I don't think that it will do me any good." I suppose that I was more than a little surprised, and even hurt, to hear that my entire course on negotiating had failed to impress him. "Why?" I asked. He explained that during his free time he invested in real estate. He would check out a neighborhood he was interested in and determine what the average market value of the homes were. Then he would pick a home he was interested in purchasing and approach the owner with an offer. He would tell the owner that he had seen all of the other homes for sale in the neighborhood and that he was willing to make a reasonable offer that was consistent with the comparables. He would also tell the seller that this offer, because it was fair, was not negotiable. Most of the time he was turned down. Occasionally, however, the owner would take the offer. The goal behind this strategy was, to use his own words, "not to have to waste all of that time negotiating."

The first and final offer is popular with people who hate to negotiate. They usually make some valuation of the product or service in question, and then make an offer that is "fair," consistent with this valuation. There is even a name for this strategy; it's called Boulwarism.

Lemuel Boulware was General Electric's senior vice-president in charge of the company's industrial relations for much of the 1950s. He formulated a negotiating strategy that was supposed to bring an end to G.E.'s troubled history of labor/management contract negotiations. Instead, his strategy made the situation worse.

Mr. Boulware had his accountants, financial advisors, labor negotiators, and other specialists put together a contract proposal that was "fair" to both labor and management. He then advised the labor union negotiators that this offer was the best he could do. In essence, he told them to take it or leave it. Mr. Boulware deadlocked, and his negotiating strategy led to a deterioration in General Electric's labor relations.

In retrospect, the reason is painfully clear. Boulwerism, in effect, forces one party to make all the concessions. If the labor union negotiators would have accepted the offer, they would have lost face and even looked inept in front of their members. In addition, even if Mr. Boulware's offer was reasonable, he would still end up looking *un*reasonable since he was insisting that the labor union make all the concessions if deadlock was to be avoided. As a result of Boulware's well intentioned but misplaced strategy, it is now presumed under federal labor law that a negotiator who opens with an offer and then refuses to make any concessions is "bargaining in bad faith."[10]

Remember, in negotiations the process is as important as the result itself. If the negotiation process is mishandled, you can end up with a situation where you have made a generous proposal to the other side only to find out they hate you for it. The fact is, people expect to negotiate, and they expect concessions to be roughly equivalent for each side. If they feel the negotiation process was unfair or especially one-sided, you can end up with a situation where they will not accept a generous offer from you, even though they may have been happy to accept it under other circumstances.

To get back to my friend who liked to invest in real estate: How did he know that he couldn't have done even better? Let's suppose he didn't care about making a better investment and his only intention was to save time by bypassing the time consuming and annoying negotiation process. The likelihood is that he was spending more time, not less, trying to get a deal closed. I am willing to bet a dollar to a dime that he spent more time walking away from deals that might have been than the average buyer actually spends negotiating a deal to close.

Four Opening Gambits

Inasmuch as your opening offer has the effect of setting the other side's expectations, a well made opening offer is crucial in order to "anchor" the other side to the result you would like them to accept. Let's go through four different opening gambits in order to see how you can set, or anchor, the other side's expectations and adjust to their pre-existing expectations.

Let us assume you are interested in purchasing a home that has an asking price of $160,000. Let's further assume that $150,000 is the target price that you would

---

[10] A friend of mine who practices labor law likes to joke that this may be the only time when it is actually illegal to open at your bottom line!

like to purchase the home for. What should your opening offer be?

Scenario 1: "Lowballing"

Even though the asking price for the home is $160,000, let's assume in this scenario that your opening offer is very low, perhaps $100,000. The theory behind this type of opening is that it puts pressure on the other side throughout the entire negotiating session. Because you have lowballed your opening offer, you can make larger concessions than the other side, while complaining about the "small" concessions they are making. This puts them on the defensive and allows you to still come out with the better end of the deal.

Unfortunately, people who lowball the other side fail to take one crucial fact into consideration: the other side's initial reaction may be hostile. If the seller perceives your opening offer to be unacceptably low—and they usually do—their reaction will most likely be to harden their negotiating position and either get upset and refuse to negotiate, or counter with a trivial concession, such as $159,500, and then dig in.

The result is a harder seller for you to deal with and a greater likelihood of deadlock. The important thing to remember is that it does not matter if your opening offer actually *is* unreasonable, it only matters that the other side *perceives* it to be an unreasonable starting point for negotiations. When negotiating, the other side's perception of reality tends to be as important as reality itself.

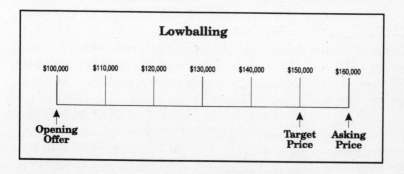

Scenario 2: Negotiating Against Your Target

In this second scenario, imagine you decide to open with an offer of $145,000 even though your goal is to purchase the home for $150,000 and the asking price is $160,000. Because you are negotiating closer to your $150,000 target than the other side is, the seller will have to make the greater number of concessions if the parties are to close at $150,000. Most likely, the other side will feel they are making more concessions than you are and that you are getting the better part of the bargain. You will tend to look stubborn or obstinate, and they may feel they are being pushed around or caused to lose face. As a result, there is a greater likelihood they will deadlock rather than close at the price of $150,000. Even if they do close at this price, there may be some effort on their part to even the score later, perhaps by refusing to act cooperatively in escrow when the transaction is actually being put together.

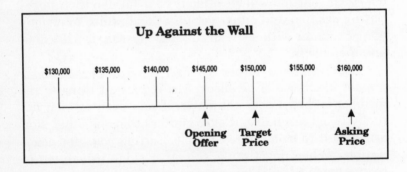

Scenario 3: "Anchoring" or "Telegraphing Your Punch"

Because the seller has an asking price of $160,000, you decide to open with an offer of $140,000 to "telegraph your punch" to the other side that you are looking to close at $150,000. This approach has a greater likelihood of success. In this scenario, the buyer can match almost any concession the seller makes with an equal concession of his own, and still arrive at an outcome of $150,000. If the seller counters with an offer of $157,000 the buyer then makes a counter of $143,000. At every stage of negotiations, the seller is reminded that an outcome of $150,000 is more and more likely to occur. The deal is "anchored."

As an approach to bargaining, anchoring has two distinct advantages. First, it creates a sense that both parties are making equal concessions. This creates the impression that the process is being handled fairly and that nobody is getting the better part of the deal. As a result, the likelihood of one party retaliating against the other by hardening their position, or by retaliating later, is diminished. Second, it sets the other side's expectations early on in the negotiating process so they become acclimated to an outcome of $150,000. This actually makes it easier to accomplish a deal at this price.

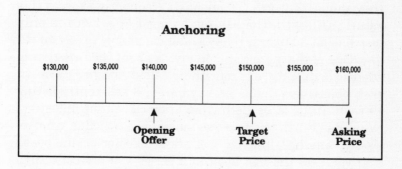

Scenario 4: "The Kiss"

This approach is similar to "anchoring," with a minor modification. Instead of anchoring by an exact amount, $140,000, the buyer makes a slightly lower offer, say $137,500. The result is that the center of gravity between the parties is no longer $150,000, but $148,750. Now the

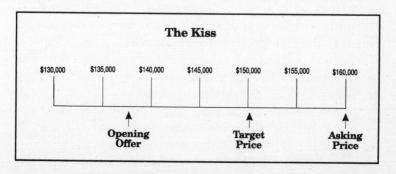

buyer can close at $150,000 while still giving the seller $1,250 (a "kiss") in additional concessions over what the seller surrendered. I find this approach to be useful in highly contentious situations where the other side's ego is engaged and they are worried about "winning" and "losing".

The Cost of Opening First

A friend of mine, who grew up on a farm in Minnesota, once told me a story about a farmer who sold a horse to a city slicker for three times what it was worth. When he was asked how he got so much money for the rather medio-cre nag, he replied: "Son, it's not what it's worth. It's what they think it's worth." Economists frequently express this same truth with the saying: "A good or service is only worth what a buyer is ready, willing, and able to pay for it."

One of the more common myths about the negotiating process is that there is something called *objective value*. In fact, objective value is an oxymoron, a self-contradicting phrase. *Value* is by definition subjective, not objective. What has worth to one person may have no value whatso-ever to another. Imagine you are a collector of fine books and you find the last book in a series you are collecting. With this volume added to your collection, the series as a whole becomes very valuable, because your collection is complete. Without it, your collection is not worth nearly as much. To the bookstore owner, however, the individual value of the book may not be great at all. She only has this one book, not the rest of the series. Her valuation of the book's worth may be based on nothing more than what she paid for it with a mark-up for profit. In this transaction, the parties' relative opinions about the books value are de-fined by their respective needs. Needless to say, if one of the parties to this transaction knows more about the other side's opinion of the value, that person will usually do bet-ter when it comes to negotiating price.

In negotiating, the most important information you can get from the other side is their *perception of value*. Do not be seduced into thinking that value is static or objec-tive. Rather than exclusively focusing on some objective assessment of what the item in question is worth, the best negotiators are also interested in the other side's perceptions. Opening first is opening blind.

The most important indicator to the other side's perception of value is their opening offer. As such, the party that makes the opening offer is usually at a disadvantage for the following reasons:

- They have communicated information about their perception of value to the other side.

- The opportunity to obtain the other side's opening offer, uninfluenced by our own, is lost.

- If you open first, the parameters of your negotiating position are automatically defined, and limited, before the other side moves.

Who usually makes the opening offer?

In general, the party that makes the opening offer is usually the party that lacks patience. Of course, there are exceptions to this rule. For example, tradition will often determine who must define their position first. If you are a car dealer, you generally have to have a sticker price in the window of every car you hope to sell. This sticker price is the first opening offer during negotiations. It defines the parameters of the seller's negotiating position, and it gives the buyer some information of the seller's perception of value. Similarly, if you are attempting to negotiate a dispute with someone, and you are the complaining party, you have an obligation to tell the other side what it is you want.

For the most part, however, the party that makes the opening offer is simply the one that lacks patience. The answer, therefore, is obvious. If there is no responsibility to make the opening offer, relax. Take your time. Try and gather information about the other side's perception of value before you move. Ask them what it is they want. The beautiful thing about most negotiators is that they cannot wait to express an opinion. Let them. And use this information to define what your counter-offer will be.

Remember, opening first is opening blind.

One Time to Open First

There is a theory that exists in certain sectors of the retail industry that argues that it is to the seller's advantage to make the opening offer in certain situations. The idea is that if the seller sets the price, the buyer will, under certain conditions, back off of the asking price by a certain amount and begin negotiating *no matter what the asking price is*. For example, if the seller asks for $5 the buyer will offer $3. If the seller asks for $10 the buyer will offer $7. And if the seller asks for $15 the buyer will offer $10. In order for this approach to work, the general consensus is that two criteria need to be present.

First, the buyer should not have any accurate idea as to what the product is worth. The moment the buyer has an idea as to what the fair market value of an item is, the ability of the seller to manipulate him by arbitrarily setting the asking price is lost. If the buyer is away from home or in a new or strange environment, it is highly likely he will not have a clear fix on local market conditions. Europeans are used to paying as much as twice what Americans pay for consumer electronic goods, such as VCRs, cameras, and CD players. As such, Europeans rarely bargain for price in stores like Circuit City, where everything tends to be at least a little bit negotiable and sometimes very negotiable, because they are pleased with the asking price. This is yet another example of how the buyer's perception of value has a tremendous impact on the negotiating session.

Second, the buyer has to be able to easily afford the item in question, or have a very high perceived need for the product. There was a story about Burt Reynolds in the San Francisco Chronicle in 1992 by the columnist Herb Caen. Apparently, Mr. Reynolds was sitting in the back of a limo driving east on California Street in San Francisco when he spotted some lithographs that he liked in the window of an art gallery. On an impulse, he ordered the limo to stop. He jumped out of the car, rushed into the art gallery, and purchased several thousands of dollars worth of artwork. Minutes later, he was back in his limo and on the road.

Obviously, spending several thousands of dollars on lithographs is far easier for Burt Reynolds than it is for the average working American. However, if the average American were on vacation in Mexico, for example, and saw a leather wallet he wanted on sale for $10 or $15, the impact of that purchase would be far less to him than it would be to the average Mexican citizen. In fact, if the American liked the wallet, the fact that it was priced at $10 or $15 would probably have very little impact on his decision to buy.

When looked at properly, this approach to setting the opening offer is no different from the concept of "anchoring." All the seller is really doing is setting the buyer's expectations with the opening offer. The fact that the buyer can easily afford the product and has a high perceived need for it gives the seller opportunities to take control of negotiations. Of course, if you are the buyer in this situation, the only remedy is to either be patient and not negotiate until you have determined the value of the product, or pay full price or more!

Capitulation (Killing the Sticker Price)

My all-time favorite car dealer story came from a young lady from Washington, D.C., who had just purchased a used car she saw advertised in the classified ads section of the Washington Post. When she arrived at the seller's home to inspect the automobile, she fell in love with the car immediately. It was immaculate. It had low mileage, performed well on the road test, had a leather interior, an alarm system, and a top-notch stereo system.

In addition to everything else, she had looked at every other car of this type and model that was advertised for sale and had seen nothing that she liked other than this car. The seller was asking for $11,000 cash. After considering the matter briefly, she told him that she was interested in the car and wanted to make an offer. "Is your $11,000 asking price firm?" she asked. "Make me an offer," he replied. "O.K.," she said, "I'll give you $8,000 for the car." "Deal!" he said. Within 15 minutes, she was driving home in her new car. For the next five days, she agonized over whether she had paid too much for the car. After all, why had he seemed so anxious to settle for what she thought was a very low offer. Maybe something was wrong with the car? Maybe it had been in an accident that he hadn't told her about. Maybe it was a lemon with a history of chronic problems that couldn't be solved. Or maybe $8,000 was simply too much to pay for a car of that model and year. The pleasure that she derived from the purchase was now adulterated by doubt.

For most of this chapter, we have been discussing the fact that the best opening offers help to set the other side's expectations. The paradox is that they should also conform, to a certain extent, with the other side's pre-existing expectations as well. If the other side is expecting to negotiate and we accept the first offer they make, they will probably think they paid too much. This can have dangerous consequences. If someone *thinks* they got taken, they will automatically look for ways to even the score or even back out of the deal.

In general, this maxim applies to any situation where you are bargaining for price and terms: *You will never get credit for concessions that are loaded into your opening offer.*

If you open conservatively and then make concessions during the negotiating process, the other side will usually leave the process feeling good about the deal and how you approached it. You will look like someone who was willing to compromise in order to bring the deal to a close. On the other hand, if you immediately accept the other side's position, and include all of the concessions you were going to make in your opening offer, these concessions may not be recognized as having much value by the other side. They will usually leave negotiations feeling they could have, and should have, done even better than they did. This can have dangerous implications down line. If the other side feels they could have done better, they are more likely to look for ways to rewrite the deal, or even back out of it later. Your relationship with the other side will now be subjected to an unnecessary strain that could have disastrous consequences. Conversely, if the other side leaves the negotiation feeling satisfied with the result as well as the process, they are more likely to be protective of the deal that they achieved and their relationship with you.

As such, always beware of accepting the other side's opening offer. If their offer is too good to turn down and you are afraid of losing an opportunity if you try to negotiate, first ask yourself:

- What impression will this give to the other side?

- Are they expecting me to negotiate?

- Will they be suspicious if I don't?

- Is a future positive relationship with them important to me?

- If I do snap at the opening offer, will they have any opportunity to back out of the deal?

Opening Offers to Avoid Making

The informal offer.
In the first year of law school a considerable amount of time is spent indoctrinating future lawyers in the meaning of a contract. A contract, we are told, consists of an offer; the acceptance of this offer; and consideration (i.e. something of value that passes between the parties). As a result, law professors love to spend a substantial amount of time ruminating over what constitutes an offer or an acceptance. As such, in law school, the distinction is constantly drawn between a *formal* and an *informal* offer or acceptance.

In negotiations, however, as a practical matter, there is absolutely no difference between a formal and informal offer. Recently, I was brought into a case that involved a utility company that was trying to negotiate an easement with the owner of a farm. About three weeks prior to the date the parties were going to sit down and negotiate, the utility company made what it called an "informal proposal" to the farmer. When the parties actually sat down to negotiate, the farmer asked the utility company to explain in greater detail what its informal proposal was all about. The farmer was then informed that since the previous proposal was only "informal" the company did not consider itself bound by it. It had since reconsidered its position and was no longer to offer the same terms. It then made a formal offer that was much less acceptable to the farmer. The result was that the farmer claimed bad faith, and the first half of the negotiations was spent arguing over whether the utility company had "reneged" or not. The upshot was that the farmer became less amenable to selling an easement to the utility company and his negotiating position stiffened.

Had the utility company simply not made any kind of statement as to what it would offer in exchange for the easement until it were actually prepared to do so, it would have found the farmer to be more receptive to the "formal" offer that it eventually made. The farmer's expectations would not have been unreasonably raised, to be dashed at the crucial moment when negotiations actually began to commence.

The "off the record" comment.

In negotiations, whether you are making an offer or not, there is no such thing as an "off the record" comment. If the other side hears it, you might as well write it in your own blood or, perhaps more appropriately, have it engraved on your tombstone. As with the informal proposal, the simple rule here is to never say anything that you haven't thought about carefully. In other words, don't open your mouth before you engage your brain. This is a common problem with American negotiators. We love to talk. In fact, we can't shut up. As such, we tend to easily overstate or understate our case, or otherwise miscommunicate our position to the other side.

The "range" offer.

I actually saw an attorney friend of mine make this mistake at the local courthouse. My friend was representing a young man who had been involved in an auto accident. His case was strong and the insurance company had indicated a willingness to settle for a "reasonable" amount. The other attorney ran into my friend in the elevator of the courthouse about two weeks before the parties were to enter into negotiations at the mandatory settlement conference.[11] He asked my friend what his client wanted. "I can't really say," my friend replied. "I haven't really discussed settlement with him as yet." "Can't you give me a ballpark range?" the other attorney asked. "After all, I need to get the insurance company mentally prepared for settlement and I can't really do that unless we have some idea of what to expect." My friend replied, "Well, my best guess is that we will be asking for between $150,000 and $175,000."

When both parties entered into formal negotiations several weeks later, my friend made an opening offer of $170,000. Needless to say, the insurance company's attorney had expected to receive an opening offer of $150,000, and negotiations immediately bogged down. The insurance company had never heard a "range offer." What its attorney heard was $150,000 and not a penny more. For the first half of the negotiations my friend was on the defensive trying to explain why he was no longer willing to consider opening at $150,000 when he was at least considering it two weeks before. He was eventually forced to make additional concessions at the opening stage of negotiations just to get the other side engaged in the process.

In general, it is useful to note that all of the above offers share a common characteristic. They are rarely well thought out, and they usually result in the other side hardening its position if they are not followed through. As such, it is best to resist the temptation to take *any* position until you are absolutely certain it is a position you are prepared to live with.

"I'll just take this back to the manager and get it approved."

These time-tested words have annoyed and frustrated car buyers since the first car was sold off a car lot at the

---

[11] A mandatory settlement conference requires both sides in a civil lawsuit to enter into settlement discussions before a judge pro tem or a magistrate. These negotiations usually occur just prior to trial. The goal is to see if the court can be freed of the cost and nuisance of an unnecessary trial. Because the court is anxious to clear its already overburdened docket of lawsuits, a tremendous amount of pressure is put on both parties to settle the case.

beginning of the 20th century. Although they create a certain level of suspicion in buyers, there are a number of reasons why no car salesperson in the world can close a deal without first taking it back to the manager.

Selling cars is a tough business. The hours are long, the profit margins are low, the salesperson is always under pressure to succeed, customers are difficult to deal with and employee turnover is high. Negotiating, to put it simply, is a pressure cooker. The likelihood that a salesperson can make a mistake in pricing a sale is high, and the corresponding damage that can be done to the dealership is significant.

As a result, auto dealerships try to provide their salespersons with a negotiating environment that is as supportive and protective as possible. In order to do this, they start off by drastically limiting the authority of their salespersons to close any deal on the lot. And one of the first things that they do to accomplish this is limit their salesperson's ability to close the deal.

All negotiators should be reluctant to negotiate with unlimited authority whenever anything important is at stake.

Limited authority is "institutionalized patience." If you don't have the ability to close a deal then it stands to reason that you can't be pressured into a bad deal. Lack of authority is, to put it simply, the ultimate protection against the hardball negotiator who uses pressure tactics and the hard sell. By limiting your authority to close the deal you provide yourself with protection from pressure tactics. (You also give yourself a way out of negotiations in which you make mistakes and severely damage your position.)

Always try to establish the other side's authority to negotiate before you begin. If you have completely committed to a deal only to find out that they still have to get that deal approved by a higher authority, you are treading on dangerous waters. Typically, what happens next is that after taking the deal "back to the manager to get it approved," the other side comes back to the table with the bad news that they cannot obtain this approval without obtaining additional concessions from you. You are now placed in the position of having to make further concessions to close the very same deal that you had already negotiated. You are placed on the defensive and are put under pressure to back off from your original deal in order to obtain closure. This tactic is particularly effective if you have invested considerable time and energy into negotiations and are anxious to bring the matter to a close. Indeed, it is commonly known by dealers that if you have spent two to three hours negotiating on a car lot, the last thing that you want to do is deadlock, go somewhere else, and begin negotiations over again from scratch.

Limit your own authority accordingly. Attempt to determine whether the other side has complete authority to negotiate the deal to close or whether they have to get the deal approved by a higher authority first. While I have no problem negotiating with someone who does not have complete authority to close, I never want to think that I have closed the deal only to find out later that negotiations are still underway. If their authority has been limited, then it is probably a good idea to limit your own accordingly. The last time that I bought a car, after the salesperson returned from the manager for the last time, I let the dealer know that I was buying the car for my wife and that this was her money. Because she was visiting her relatives in Los Angeles, I had to get her approval in order to close the deal. I asked to use his phone to make sure that the deal was acceptable to her before I closed it. The salesman was, to put it mildly, shocked at this turn of events and told me that he felt I had not been dealing fairly with him! I assured him that this wasn't the case and called to his attention the fact that, just as she needed approval from a higher authority, so did I. Apparently, it is fine for them to limit their authority, but not for the buyer to do the same thing!

Chapter Five

Status and
The Negotiator

How to Determine Your Status

Negotiators rarely enter into negotiations with equal power. In almost every situation, one negotiator has more power than the other. This disproportionate power can have a dramatic impact not only on the outcome of negotiations but on how the parties behave during the negotiation process. If, for example, you are negotiating for a raise with your boss, the impact your departure would have on you and your boss tends to have a significant impact on how well you come out of the negotiations, as well as how you and your boss handle the negotiating process. If, for example, there are 3,500 people who would just love to have your job, chances are you will be somewhat deferential to the old man when you pop the question! On the other hand, if you are the only person that is capable of filling the position, you are probably going to be a little more forthright about how you feel.

In general, powerful negotiators usually share the following traits:

The needs of the high status negotiator tend to be more important that the other side's. During negotiations, parties tend to focus on addressing the more powerful negotiator's needs rather than the needs of the weaker negotiator. Again, a good example of this is the relationship between a person who is interviewing for a job and the potential employer. In most cases, the job seeker is concerned with demonstrating that she can meet the needs of the company better than any competing job seeker. Similarly, the prospective employer is also concerned that the employee will meet the needs of the company. Another example is the relationship between buyer and seller. In almost every sale, the vendor is concerned with demonstrating that the product she has to sell will meet the needs of the buyer better than any competing alternative. When this dynamic is present, you may be assured that the buyer is most likely the negotiator with the most power at the table. In short, if your needs are the dominant issue in a given negotiation, you probably hold the greater negotiating power.

The consequences of deadlock are usually worse for the low status negotiator. High status negotiators usually suffer fewer negative consequences from a deadlock than the other side, so they can more easily run the risk of deadlock. This tends to give them more patience while the low status negotiator is experiencing an anxiety to close. The interesting thing about this aspect of status is that the negotiator's high or low position is often a matter of perception. In a seminar I gave several years ago, a lady told me she felt helpless whenever she entered a car lot, because she knew she needed the car, while they didn't need to sell it to her. No matter how hard I tried, I couldn't convince her that the truth was the consequences of deadlock were almost always far more severe for the seller than they were for the buyer. If she would have taken this into account, and changed her perception, she would have realized that she, not the dealer, was the high status negotiator.

High status negotiators usually have better alternatives to negotiating than the other side does. This is actually the acid test for determining what your status is relative to the other side's. If your alternatives to negotiating are better than the other side's, you will be hurt less by a deadlock. When I purchased my last home, I was buying in what was a clear buyer's market. While there were not many homes on the market, it was still winter and a large number of homes were expected to be listed for sale in the late spring or early summer. The sellers of the home that I was interested in had already begun building a new home, and they expected to see construction completed within a few months. As such, come Hell or high water, they were going to be moving whether their existing home had sold or not. To make matters worse, their present home had been on the market for nine months and we were the first serious buyers to make an offer. We, on the other hand, were in no hurry to purchase. We had only just begun checking out the market and expected to spend at least three or four months getting a feel for what was out there before we began to seriously look for an opportunity. While my wife and I were intrigued by this house, we weren't worried about not getting it. Needless to say, the consequences of a deadlock had different significances to each party's attitude to negotiations throughout the entire process.

Low status negotiators often face immediate deadlines. Any number of factors can influence the alternatives either party has, but the deadlines the parties are facing are a sure tip-off. If one side has an immediate deadline that only a successful negotiation can address, then that negotiator is in a classic low status position. Conversely, if you have no deadline to worry about, you will probably be negotiating from a position of strength. This is why project managers should always negotiate for resources before they agree to undertake the job. Once you agree to do a job, you are trapped. If you then try to get additional personnel, budget allocations, or other resources, you will have a hard time. Your leverage is lost because you now have project deadlines that have to be met.

In order to determine your relative status, ask yourself the following questions:

- Who has better alternatives to negotiating?

- Who will be harmed more by a deadlock?

- Whose "needs" will the parties be focusing on during negotiations? If one party's needs predominate, to what extent will this influence our negotiations?

- Is either party facing a deadline?

Why Sellers Bow Deeper
(and What They Do About It)

When a friend of mine first started practicing law in Southern California, he was placed under the watchful and occasionally benevolent eye of a partner who specialized in dealing with the Japanese. "When dealing with the Japanese," he told my friend, "always know your status."

In Western societies, when we interact with people we tend to treat each other as equals. Employees commonly address their immediate superiors by their first names, and personal relationships tend to be informal and relaxed. This is especially true in the United States where many of the class distinctions of the Old World, such as titles, class accents, and separate educational systems for the aristocracy, have been dropped in favor of a more egalitarian approach to life. We even have the concept set forth in the opening lines of our nation's Declaration of Independence (". . . all men are created free and equal . . .")

In Japan, as in all societies oriented by the philosophical tenants of Confucius, nobody is equal. You are either an elder brother or a younger brother, a child or a parent, a student or a teacher, an employee with higher or lower ranking, greater or lesser seniority. In short, every relationship and every person tends to be defined in terms of status.

When a Japanese buyer and seller meet, the buyer clearly has higher status. The seller makes a deeper bow in order to reflect the buyer's higher status.[12] And, not coincidentally, the buyer is expected to, and usually does, get the "edge" in the transaction.

The purchaser's higher status is a fact of life in the

---

[12] Bowing is what anthropologists call a "high context" ritual, a concept developed by Edward T. Hall. When people communicate in a high context manner, they search for meaning and understanding in more than just the words that are spoken between them. Body language, subtle expressions, inferences of meaning, and sometimes circuitous ways of getting to the point are typical in high context communications. America is a good example of a low context culture. In the United States, almost all of the meaning that is to be found during any communication is to be found in the spoken words between the parties. Low context communicators tend to believe in "saying what they mean" or "putting their cards on the table." They see things in black and white terms and are easily confused or misled by subtle or otherwise ambiguous behavior.

West as well. But the reasons for it are economical, not cultural. We may use different expressions ("the customer is always right") and body language to express it, but it has a direct impact on how the negotiation process unfolds.

Put simply, buyers have higher status simply because sellers' markets are short lived in a competitive free market. Since most products are sold in a buyer's market, the seller is more dependent on the buyer than the buyer is on any one particular seller. The Mazda Miata is a perfect example of this. Several years ago, when the Miata was first released, you couldn't get one unless you waited six to nine weeks, paid more than full price, and took whatever color they wanted to give you. A friend of mine asked how he could negotiate the purchase of one of these cars. "You can't," I told him. "It's a seller's market. But if you're patient," I continued, "wait one year. It will be a buyer's market again and they will negotiate with you." Sure enough, after one year, production rose to meet demand, higher inventory levels began to accumulate, and the dealerships began to negotiate.

Buyers start off with more power

The fact that the buyer has higher status than the seller has important implications for the negotiation process. Buyers can be tactical, and they usually are when they are actively bargaining. They can revisit settled issues, demand unilateral concessions, complain about the price, procrastinate, and even walk out, confident that the seller will usually grin and bear it.

In addition to market conditions, there are several reasons why the buyer's initial bargaining power is usually greater than the seller's.

First, the needs of the buyer tend to be more important than the needs of the seller. Indeed, the entire focus of the negotiations between buyer and seller tend to be dominated by the seller trying to convince the buyer why he needs the product in question. The buyer's focus is the same: "Why should I buy? Why does this product address my needs better than any other?" This gives the buyer momentum and a certain degree of control, because it places the burden of proof on the seller. The seller has to convince the buyer to buy. The buyer rarely has to convince the seller to sell.

Buyers usually have better alternatives to negotiating than sellers. Almost every seller has competition. This gives the buyer alternatives the seller rarely enjoys. As such, if the buyer and seller deadlock, the buyer can simply go to one of the seller's competitors to rescue the situation. This is especially true on a car lot. If you don't like what a particular dealer offers, simply go to another dealership selling the same automobiles, and you can start over again without suffering any penalty from your previous deadlock.

The consequences of deadlock are usually worse for the seller. The whole point behind being a salesperson is to close the deal. If the deal isn't closed, the transaction is, from the seller's perspective, a failure. As such, it is almost always the seller's duty and burden to keep the buyer engaged in the negotiating process. The buyer then has the ability to extract concessions from the seller in exchange for simply agreeing to stay engaged in the process. Again, this tends to give the buyer momentum and control.

How sellers deal with the buyer's status

Sellers must try to avoid tactical behavior whenever possible for fear that it will disengage the buyer from the process and delay, or even prevent closing the deal. Almost every sales seminar I know of emphasizes the importance of getting closure on the deal before the interaction is terminated. The worst words a seller can hear from the prospective buyer is: "I'll need some time to think about it."

Tactical behavior by the seller also runs a higher risk of backfiring and can actually make the buyer a tougher negotiator to deal with. Think about it. If you feel that a car dealer is "taking" you, how do you react? You may give in, but not without some sense of bitterness. The more usual reaction is to stall or even disengage from the negotiating process and look for another dealer.

Sellers may respond to the fact they lack status in one of four ways.

First, sellers will try to avoid having to negotiate at all. Because the seller lacks status, negotiating almost always "costs" him in terms of some reduction in price or "free" addition to their product or service. Sellers use a number of different approaches to accomplish this, including developing a personal relationship with the purchaser in order to reduce his defensiveness, and "end-running" the purchasing departments of companies entirely by dealing exclusively with the end user.[13]

Second, effective sellers gather as much information as they can before making any concessions. Anyone who has ever purchased a car has been subjected to this approach. From the moment you first meet the dealer, you are being asked a variety of questions designed to determine your price flexibility, the type of purchaser you are—tough or manageable—when you need the product, and the minimum product you will settle for. Questions like "Where do you work?", "What do you do for a living?", "Where do you live?", and "Do you want to pay cash or finance the purchase?" are designed to give the dealer information about your income level. If the dealer asks the buyer when he purchased his last new car, he obtains valuable information about what the buyer really wants out of the transaction. If the customer bought his last new car three years ago, he is probably more focused on quality, as opposed to just price, than if he purchased his last new car 10 years ago. Owners who hold onto cars longer and drive them until they are ready to retire tend to focus more on cost.

Third, sellers have a system that is set up to deal with their buyers. This system of negotiating is well thought out, rigidly adhered to, and constantly rehearsed. It is designed to take full advantage of the one "edge" the seller enjoys. The buyer is purchasing on the seller's "turf". As such, the dealership gives the seller any backup or support that will increase his bargaining power. Watch what hap-

---

[13] The "end-run" involves finding the end-users of the product or service to be sold and selling it to them first. The purchasing department, whose buyers are actually trained to negotiate price and terms, is now reduced to the ineffective position of merely filling orders. They lack the power to negotiate, because the sale was already made in their absence.

pens if a salesperson's deal begins to go sour. Automatically, new faces begin to appear, usually more experienced salespersons take over, and new approaches are tried out. In time, this system usually shifts power between the parties giving the seller opportunities to control the process.

Fourth, the seller always knows when to say "yes" and when to deadlock. Having a clear sense of objectivity is crucial for negotiators who are weak or negotiating under pressure. Sometimes the urge to close the deal and lock it down is so great, sellers get taken in the process. The decision on when to deadlock is so important to car dealerships, they usually refuse to give salespersons the power to close. Every salesperson must "take it back to the manager to get it approved" before the deal can close. Because the manager is not directly involved in the pressure cooker called "negotiating," he tends to be less emotionally involved and more objective.

Chapter Six

Buyer vs. Seller

If you really want to know how to buy anything, don't go to a purchasing seminar. Go to the best sales seminar you can find, and learn how products and services are sold to you. Within a short period of time, you will learn that sellers suffer from an obsession. To put it simply, "closing the deal" is the only thing they care about. Buy any sales book, listen to any sales tape, or go to any sales seminar, and you will notice that the entire subject seems to be focused on how to get the buyer to agree to "close." As a result, sellers' seminars tend to focus on persuasion and influence skills that are focused on closing, as well as on a variety of different closing tactics.

The strength of this obsession tends to increase during the negotiating process. The closer the seller gets to closing the deal, the greater the obsession over closing becomes. At some point, the desire to close becomes so great, it affects the seller's negotiating ability. This is often the greatest single advantage the buyer has. Indeed, at the point just before the buyer says, "I'll take it," the seller is usually seriously weak and impatient.

Nibbling the Seller's Soft Underbelly

The most effective tactic any buyer can use at this stage of negotiating is called "nibbling." "Nibbling" simply means getting a small edge at the closing stages of the negotiation. The philosophy behind it is that effective negotiating is simply getting "an edge," say an extra two or three percent, and getting it *consistently* on each and every deal you negotiate. Because the buyer has the higher status at the table, nibbling is a very easy tactic to succeed at if you simply pay attention to the fundamentals.

So how does one nibble? It is really very simple and often painless for both parties. Successful nibbling is accomplished by simply following seven points.

1. *Nibbling must be done at the end of the negotiating process when the seller is losing patience.* Nibbling during the middle of any negotiating process is not nibbling. It's negotiating. Be patient and wait until you have almost, but not quite, reached that magic moment of closure. This is when the seller is at his weakest point of resisting any concession you request.

2. *The buyer must ask for a small concession.* It need be no more than one or two percent of the purchase price. Don't reopen the entire negotiation process. The whole point behind the nibble is to get a small extra before closing, not to gouge your seller and threaten to delay, or even derail, the entire process.

3. *The nibble must be easily conceded by the seller.* This is not necessarily the same thing as saying that the nibble must be small in relation to the purchase price. An example of an easily surrendered nibble is an extra feature sold at cost, so that the buyer gains and the seller suffers no loss.

4. *The nibble should be offered as a condition for closing the deal.* This means you nibble only once and, in doing so, you give the seller a strong carrot to surrender the nibble. Tell the seller that if she grants you this one small concession, you will close the deal right then and there. This has the impressive effect of presenting your seller with a dilemma: Does she risk losing the "close" over a small concession that is relatively painless to surrender? Probably not, especially if she intends doing business for any length of time!

5. *The nibble should* not *be price related.* This is the easiest way to guarantee the nibble will be accepted and your adversary will lack the patience to

resist it. This is because price—the amount of cash the seller takes back to her company—is one of the key measures by which the seller gauges her success at the negotiating table. As such, whenever a buyer attempts to reduce the price, and limit the amount of cash the seller receives, he creates resistance in the seller. On the other hand, if you ask for extras, slightly higher quality goods or services, warranty or service agreements, or slightly earlier delivery or performance, the seller is more inclined to make the concession, since the cost of the concession to the seller is less than the benefit of the concession is to the buyer. The reason is that most extras, warranties and service agreements are subjected to a very high mark-up, allowing the seller to give concessions that are relatively cost-free to the seller while being of greater benefit to the buyer. A good example of this is floor mats. The dealer mark-up on an item like this is tremendous, sometimes as much as two or three hundred percent. As such, if the dealer throws in the floor mats for free, the actual cost to the dealer is the amount that the dealer paid—perhaps only a few dollars. The benefit to the buyer, however, is always going to be measured by what the buyer would have had to pay had the buyer purchased them at the retail price. Hence, the benefit to the buyer is greater than the cost is to the seller.

6. *The nibble must be justified as necessary or significant to your decision to buy.* Don't just ask for a nibble to get an "edge." Make sure your request has a logical relationship to your needs. For example, if, in the process of purchasing a laser printer, you note that you are intending to use the printer for desktop publishing and that without soft fonts you have no rationale for making the purchase, you have provided the seller with a powerful incentive for making the concession. If, on the other hand, the seller senses that you are simply trying to get an extra that you don't really need, the seller is go-

ing to be more inclined to resist. Remember, by justifying your request, you are putting the ball firmly in the other side's court, and making it harder for them to resist.

7. *Prepare your nibble in advance.* Don't make your tactics up as you go along. It will look contrived, and you will not be prepared to justify it in terms of your needs. Think ahead of time, and ask yourself the following questions:

- What do I need to make it work? Service agreements, power supplies, cables, toner, warranties?

- What do I need to make it work better? Peripherals, software, upgrades?

- What goods or services are of slightly higher quality?

- What extras match the product and my needs?

Loss Leaders

Several years ago, a major software company decided to sell a word processing program that had been priced at $400.00, for just $99. The goal was to encourage otherwise reticent buyers to "test drive" the program and see what a superior product it was. Later on, when upgrades or new versions were released, the company hoped that these users would buy the new product at the previously high price, instead of the new discounted price. It never happened. The software never sold for more than the discounted price of $99.

As a sales strategy, "loss leaders" rarely work. The "loss leader" is a pricing strategy whereby the seller gives the buyer a significant discount on the first sale of the good or service in question, with the expectation that after the buyer has seen what a fine product he has purchased, he will return and continue to buy more at full price. This rarely happens. In fact, this strategy is called "loss leaders" because it is the leading way to make losses.

When people purchase a product at a low price, their opinions on its value are almost always readjusted. Once this occurs, it is very difficult to readjust their perception of value to the previously high price again. In fact, when loss leaders are given at the beginning of a buyer-seller relationship, two things inevitably occur.

First, the loss leader usually results in the cheapening of the value of the seller's product. The result can be disastrous. If the software is sold at a reduced price for only $99, the buyer will come away from the transaction with the opinion that the software is only "worth" $99. This also has the effect of cheapening other products or services similar in nature.

Second, a precedent has been set for future dealings between the parties. The buyer may begin to expect similar discounts on other products or services. This can create a situation where the seller is forced to engage in unnecessary haggling with his buyers. The end result can be a strained relationship with the buyer and an unnecessary discounting of the seller's other products.

There are certain occasions when loss leaders do constitute an acceptable pricing strategy, particularly if the seller has no intention of maintaining the higher price in any case. If the regular price is legitimate, however, the loss leader can only undermine it and create problems for the seller.

If you are the buyer in this situation, relax. When the seller later attempts to raise the price of the product, ask the seller to justify the price increase and negotiate. With very few exceptions, the seller will make additional concessions in order to close the deal. While loss leaders are the leading way of making losses for sellers, they are a wonderful opportunity for buyers to permanently lower the price of a product.

The "Straw Man"

The "straw man" is a very effective buyer's tactic. It tests the seller's price while lowering his expectations as to what he hopes to receive on the sale.

Imagine you see a piece of antique furniture advertised in the classified section of your local newspaper. Let's assume the seller is asking $500 for the furniture. On the first day the ad runs, he receives a phone call from a would-be buyer offering him $200 for the furniture. He turns it down. Then he receives a second call from another buyer offering him $150. He turns it down. Then he gets a third call from yet another buyer offering $275. He turns it down as well. All day long, he receives offers from buyers, all within the range of $150-$300, but none higher. Furthermore, everyone remarks that the furniture is beautiful, but it is priced too high. Finally, the seller begins to worry. Did he price the furniture too high? Perhaps he set his expectations too high. Maybe he should have taken the previous offer for $275 rather than turn it down. Perhaps an opening offer of $400 would have been more appropriate. Just as he is about to change the classified ad, he receives an offer from a new buyer offering to pay $400 for the furniture. He snaps it up.

What the seller didn't know was that all of the other phone calls he received that day were made by friends of the last caller. Their role was to frighten the seller into thinking he was asking far too much for the furniture and its real value was in the range of $200 to $300. Thus, when the last caller offered him $400, he snapped it up without negotiating further.

Seller's Closing Tactics

The problem with closing tactics is that they are based on the theory that the seller can successfully manipulate, or even intimidate, the buyer into agreeing to the deal. That would be fine if it weren't for the fact that most people know when they are being manipulated and resent it. The result is that the buyer becomes suspicious of the seller's motives, justifiably in most cases, and tends to disengage from the negotiation process. As a result, most successful sales and marketing professionals tend to use closing tactics sparingly, if at all, when trying to make a sale with an important customer. After all, if the closing tactic is obvious, it may alienate the customer. And if they alienate the customer, they may lose the entire relationship, not just the single sale.

The best sellers are those who take a low key approach, gather information about the buyer's needs and realize their status is low. This is not what sellers want to hear. Selling is such a tough job, salespersons are always looking for some "approach" to help them close deals. A large number of corporate trainers make a lot of money telling salespersons what they want to hear rather than the truth: Selling is never easy unless the product sells itself. Selling is as much luck and trial-and-error as anything else. The best salespersons are those who work long hours, take risks and hear "no" over and over and over. No gimmick will ever make selling easy.

Nevertheless, closing tactics still seem to be used by many salespersons who are not really concerned with maintaining a positive relationship with the buyer. If the sale is a one shot deal, or if circumstances are such that the relationship between the parties is already strained, the following closing tactics will probably pop up at one point or another.

The soft fluffy kitten close.

Any pet store owner will tell you that if you want to sell a cute kitten, lend it to the customer on a trial basis and then, when the trial period ends, bill them promptly. The underlying theory for this close is that it is harder to return something you already have than to refuse to buy something you don't have. This is why advertisements for products on television usually offer you a money back guarantee within a certain period of time if you aren't satisfied with the product. The truth is, once someone has taken possession of something, they rarely return it. Rarely.

The trial run close.

This close is used in transactions involving the continuing or ongoing sale of products or services, such as magazine subscriptions or bottled water delivered to your house. With the trial run, the seller offers a special introductory rate for new subscribers. The product's price usually expires within a designated period of time; the shorter the period, the better, or the buyer may get used to the low price.

The alternatives close.

Instead of asking if you want to buy, the seller merely assumes he has successfully closed and moves on to the next stage. "Do you want to charge it or pay cash?" or "Shall we deliver or will you pick up?"

Sometimes the alternatives close is based on the assumption that you want to close but you don't know exactly what you are going to buy: "Would you prefer the standard or the upgraded model?"

On other occasions, the seller intentionally misstates the order in order to confirm it. If, for example, the seller wanted to sell you 10 widgets, instead of the five you requested, he would ask: "Did you say you wanted 100 widgets delivered or 10?"

In either case, the purpose of the alternatives close is to rush the buyer into making the decision to buy without further reflection.

The "Amen" close.

This closing tactic is based on getting the buyer into the habit of agreeing with the seller and saying "yes" to every question he poses. Of course, in order for the tactic to work, each question must be phrased to elicit a "yes" response.

Seller: "You said you are dissatisfied with the product you are presently using?"

Buyer: "Yes"

Seller: "And you like the features that our product has?"

Buyer: "Yes"

Seller: "And you like our unconditional guarantee?"

Buyer: "Yes"

Seller: "And you like our price?"

Buyer: "Yes"

Seller: "Is tomorrow a good day for us to deliver the product to you?"

Buyer: "Yes"

Of course, if the buyer says "no," the seller usually expresses surprise and asks: "Is there anything that I have missed?"

The deadline close.

This tactic tries to create a sense of panic in the mind of the buyer so he will close without thinking about it further. Phrases like "Act now!" and "This offer is limited!" are more focused on taking advantage of a tendency to impulse buy than anything else. Other examples of the deadline close include the following approaches:

- "You know, there was another buyer here this morning looking at this car. He said he was probably coming back tomorrow to buy it. I doubt I'll see another one of these models on the lot for some time to come."

- "Our prices will be going up tomorrow. If you want to lock in a low price, you'd better act now."

This tactic is especially hardball and results in deadlock as often as not.

Guilt and fear.

Anyone who has ever purchased life insurance has been subjected to this tactic. The object of the tactic is to force the buyer into closing the deal by installing a sense of guilt or fear into the buyer if they don't buy.

- "Do you know how your wife and children would feel if you died without insurance?"

- "Don't you owe it to your daughter to buy a car that would completely protect her in an accident?"

- "We have been friends for a long time and you know that I am always concerned with selling you a quality product."

Get It Cheaper In The City

My friends in Northern California are always surprised to discover they can usually purchase a new automobile for as much as a thousand dollars less if they simply buy it in Los Angeles. I purchased a 1988 Mercury Sable in Los Angeles for $1,500 less than the lowest price I could get on any car lot in northern California. Why? For the same reason that retail prices in metropolitan areas tend to be less than retail prices in surrounding rural areas. There are more people living in Los Angeles than in the bay area of northern California. Whenever you have a large number of people living in one area, there tend to be more stores, with larger inventory levels and lower overhead rates per product. This results in cheaper prices.

The prices of almost all products are driven as much by the geographical area in which they are sold as by the base cost of the product itself. While I do not recommend driving 300 miles to the nearest megalopolis to purchase your groceries, I do recommend the drive if you are purchasing an expensive item that will have a significant impact on your pocketbook. Cars, boats, high-end consumer electronics, computers, or any other "durable" that involves enough money to justify a payment plan will fall into this category.

Chapter Seven

The Power of Information

I gave a seminar recently to some employees of a large Japanese corporation that had set up regional headquarters in the United States. One of the executives of that company complained that whenever he sent a proposal to Japan, they always replied by asking him "why." He would provide his best rationale for his position and send it to Japan, only to receive another reply asking more questions and requesting more information. After sending five replies and receiving five more requests for information, he became convinced that they were simply shining him on and not taking him seriously. In fact, they were not.

The Japanese are masters at the art of gathering information before they negotiate or decide anything. In part, this is the result of their reluctance to make mistakes and thereby lose face among their colleagues.[14] It is also due to the fact that the Japanese are an especially risk-averse, conservative people that prefer the sure thing to the speculative bet. Westerners, on the other hand, are less worried about risk, so they are more likely to make decisions or take positions on the spur of the moment. We tend to make it up as we go along. In fact, it is typical for an American negotiator to walk into a room, sit down, and open with a demand or an opening offer without attempt-

[14] Drawing attention to oneself is the easiest way to set yourself up for a fall in Japan. This is true whether you are, in effect, bragging about your accomplishments, or, even worse, if you have made a mistake that is known to your colleagues or superiors. The Japanese have a saying that expresses this rather well: "The nail that sticks up gets hammered down."

ing to gather any information in advance about the people she is negotiating with, their perception of value, their deadlines, or other information that could have a dramatic outcome on the negotiations.

The More You Know Now, The Less You'll Have to Find Out Later

In fact, information is the most powerful asset any negotiator can have. The negotiator who focuses on gathering information before deciding makes few mistakes, almost always is able to exploit the weakness of the other side, and is rarely fooled or taken in by the other side. Information can be divided into three general categories:

- Information about the other negotiator
- Information about our position
- Information about the other side's perceptions and position

Information about the other negotiator.
    If you are dealing with an individual, learn as much about the other negotiator as you can before negotiations commence. Attempt to discover his status inside his own company or group; what his authority to negotiate is (Can he cut the deal alone, or does someone else has to approve it?); how he has negotiated in previous negotiations; and what his negotiating "pattern" or method is. In addition to business information, note the other side's birth dates, anniversaries, favorite wines, dietary habits, religious beliefs, hobbies, children's names, and so on. This personal information can be used as an ice breaker or to help you avoid embarrassing mistakes.

When you are dealing with someone who is negotiating on behalf of an organization, you should attempt to gather information about the organization itself, in addition to the individual you are dealing with. Develop files on the organizations you do business with regularly, and keep those files up to date. Public sources of information about organizations include *Standard & Poors*, credit checks, *Moody's*, shareholder reports, clipping services, press releases, corporate organization charts, and data base services. If you are negotiating in a commercial setting, get in the habit of visiting the other side's plant or place of business. This helps you accomplish two objectives: one, to familiarize yourself with the other side's facilities and business; and two, to develop personal relationships with other people inside the company other than just the person you are negotiating with.

Information about your position.

By making these decisions *before* you walk into the negotiating room, you have a better chance of acting rationally, not emotionally. Ask yourself: When do I deadlock? What are the consequences of a deadlock? What is the cost of a deadlock to me? What are my alternatives to negotiating? Do I have alternatives to negotiating that are especially attractive? What are my real underlying needs? What justification will I provide for the positions I take in these negotiations? What is my negotiation target or goal? What external pressures affect my negotiability? Can I deal with or control these factors in advance? What is my deadline? Can this deadline be changed? What are the consequences of my failing to meet this deadline?

Information about the other side's perception and position.

Try to state the other side's position better than they can. Don't just focus on their weaknesses. What are the strong points of their position? How will you deal with these arguments? What justification can you provide for your position in meeting these arguments? What is their deadline? Sellers love to ask buyers, "When do you need it?" in order to determine this. Be aware of personal deadlines, such as weekends or personal commitments, as well as institutional deadlines, such as "just in time" inventory deadlines and project management deadlines. Why are they negotiating? What brought them to the table? Are they accountable to any other person that has a stake in these negotiations? Have they been involved in previous negotiations of a similar sort? With whom? What concessions did they make? What positions did they take? What are their real underlying needs, as opposed to the demands they are making or positions they are taking? If you know their needs, you almost always have control of the process. Do they have authority to close the deal? If not, why not? Who has it? If they are selling, who is their competition?

Silence is Golden

People are like radio stations. They can't handle ten seconds of dead air without broadcasting. Silence is a devastatingly effective negotiating tactic if you are dealing with someone who can't shut up. In fact, the best negotiators are those who only talk 40 percent of the time. They are not afraid to let the other side dominate the conversation. Not only do they tend to gather more information from the other side than they surrender, but they also avoid making unnecessary mistakes.

Furthermore, when they do speak, they usually speak to gather information. The best negotiators are those who regularly ask the other side questions, give them options to consider, and work to actively ferret out information from the other side.

If the other side wants to say something, *don't interrupt*. Let them talk themselves dry. Whenever they take a position or make a demand, get in the habit of asking them what their justification or need is for such a concession. Follow up with as many questions as you can reasonably ask. Remember, in the negotiating game, information equals power.

Never Ask Close-Ended Questions
Unless You Already Know the Answer

Close-ended questions call for a yes or no answer. The problem with close ended questions is you may get an answer from the other side that you don't like. This answer now becomes a "position." Of course, once the other side takes a position, they will tend to harden and defend it. Furthermore, if the question is embarrassing, or requires the other side to reassess or change their position, a close-ended question is more likely to elicit a dishonest answer.

Probably the most telling part of the William Kennedy Smith rape trial was when the district attorney, Moira Lasch, questioned prospective jury members. The difference between how she questioned the jury and how Mr. Smith's attorney questioned the jury was remarkable. Ms. Lasch repeatedly asked closed-ended questions such as: "Can you be a fair and impartial juror?" and "Can you be impartial no matter how you feel personally about the Kennedys?" What did she expect them to say? "No?" I've seen lawyers do this repeatedly. The last time was during a trial in Palo Alto, California, when I was trying a case against an individual who was Iranian. The Iranian's attorney repeatedly kept asking the jurors, "Are you a racist? Are you prejudiced against Iranians? Can you be an impartial juror even though my client is an Iranian?" I felt like jumping up and shouting, "Even if they are racists, do you really expect them to admit it?"

If you want an honest answer, ask an open-ended question. An open-ended question never calls for a yes or no answer. Open-ended questions always call for a narration. Instead of asking if a juror was a racist, the attorney should have told the juror a story and asked him what he would have done in that situation. For example, a good open-ended way of asking if someone was prejudiced would go like this: "How do you feel about Iranians? Have you ever known any Iranians before? What was your relationship with them like?"

Open-ended questions usually begin with the newspaper reporter's questions: Who, what, when, where, why, and how.

Good examples of open-ended questions include:

What would you like for this product?

What if I were to give you this concession? Could you offer me another concession in return?

How does this concession meet your needs?

Why do you need this concession?

Chapter Eight

On Intimidation

The Ultimate Intimidation Tactic

The most intimidating thing that you can do to intimidate someone who is trying to intimidate you by using intimidation tactics is not to be intimidated. It's intimidating!

If someone uses hardball tactics during negotiations, the worst thing that you can do is to react positively or negatively. If you react positively, you will simply get more hardball behavior. Conversely, if you react negatively by retaliating or using your own hardball tactics, you merely escalate the conflict. This only gets both parties' egos engaged and heightens the possibility of deadlock.

The best reaction is no reaction at all. If you don't get hard, or soft, if you don't make concessions or escalate, they will begin to wonder just what it is that you know. You will appear confident and in control. The irony is, they will end up being the party that is intimidated, not you!

Zen and the Art of Negotiating

"Don't just do something," Buddha said. "Stand there." Only one person can determine whether an intimidation tactic or a power play will work in any negotiation. That is the person against whom it is being used. If the other side throws a temper tantrum and you give concessions in order to bring it to an end, you can only expect to get one thing during the balance of the negotiating session—more temper tantrums. You decide whether their power play works, not them.

Once you decide not to reward intimidation tactics, it's a whole new ball game. It is an axiom of military science that in battle, you only fight effective maneuvers. You never try to stop your enemy from engaging in an ineffective maneuver. Similarly, if their tactics are ineffective (and, as we have already noted, whether their tactics work is *our* decision, not theirs) the best course of action is simply to sit back, do nothing, and let them play themselves out. If the intimidation tactic is ineffective, there is no reason to expend your energy in trying to stop it.

The Negotiator's Sucker Punch

"You can do better than that." These words are used by a negotiator who wants to watch you negotiate against yourself. A common tactic used by hardball negotiators is to argue about any position you take without offering a counter-offer to it. This almost always occurs at the outset of negotiations. The longer both sides argue over the reasonableness of our offer, the more pressure is put on us to make additional back-to-back concessions.

Negotiation must be a process of reciprocity if it is to work. If you are the only one making concessions at the outset of negotiations, there is a high probability you will be "taken" or you will eventually deadlock. Once you give two concessions in a row, the other side invariably demands three. At some point, you have to put your foot down and insist the other side gets engaged in the process. And the best time to put your foot down is at the outset of negotiations, not later on.

Once you make an offer which they refuse to accept, ask for a counter-offer. If they feel your opening position is unreasonable, ask them what they think is reasonable. Insist they get engaged in the process. This is important for two reasons. First, when you make an offer, you have given the other side important information about your perception of value. You have also defined the parameters of your negotiating position. If you then make additional concessions before they define their position, you are negotiating "blind," without information, and this makes you an especially weak negotiator. Second, when you make back-to-back concessions, you set a precedent for your continuing to do so. The other side will actually harden their position, not soften it, and this will increase the potential for deadlock.

Chapter Nine

And Finally . . .

A Word on Lawyers and Negotiating

Lawyers are lousy negotiators. It hurts me to say this, but it's true. I have been a lawyer for over 14 years now. Over that period of time, I have negotiated everything from the settlement of civil disputes to the negotiation of lease agreements. I have handled the dissolution of partnerships, the mergers and acquisitions of corporations, the adjusting of tax obligations, and the sale of businesses in divorce cases. While attorneys have many uses, negotiating the resolution of disputes is not one of them. If you need to sue someone, to figure out what the appropriate level of child support is in a custody dispute, to create a lease agreement, or to incorporate a business, by all means, hire a lawyer. If, on the other hand, you want to preserve a relationship instead of destroying it, to resolve a dispute without losing a friendship, or to save your marriage instead of dissolving it, think long and hard before you get a lawyer involved.

It has been my experience that when lawyers negotiate for their clients, they tend to cause as many problems as they solve. This is not to say they don't solve problems. Lawyers are very good at telling you what the law is and enforcing that law when you need to. They are also good at writing contracts, drafting lease agreements, or preparing wills and trusts for your family.

For the most part, however, if you get an attorney involved in the early stages of a dispute, the likelihood that the dispute will get worse instead of better is very high.

Lawyers, especially trial lawyers, are classic hardball negotiators. They *routinely* threaten each other, engage in brinkmanship, escalate conflicts, disengage unnecessarily from the negotiation process, send hostile letters back and forth (so-called "paper wars"), and use a vast array of other intimidation tactics as a normal part of their practice of law. In fact, the deterioration of civility between attorneys has become so commonplace, it has caused, in the words of Scott Turow, a "malaise" to set in over the entire practice of law.[15]

Think before you engage an attorney

Ask yourself, "Why am I hiring this attorney?" Lawyers are excellent technicians of the law; they are essential for the drafting of contracts, structuring tax shelters, or setting up businesses. They are also essential advocates. If you are suing someone, or being sued, and you don't have an attorney, you are crazy. There is an old saying that the person who represents himself in court has a fool for an attorney. It's that simple. However, you should think long and hard before you get lawyers unnecessarily involved in negotiations. There are a number of reasons why.

Lawyers are like rabbits; they have a nasty habit of multiplying. The mere presence of an attorney in a negotiation is intimidating. The result is predictable. If you bring your lawyer to the table, the other side will insist on bringing their lawyer. Now the lawyers begin to control the process, with predictable results!

A lawyer's knowledge is limited to the practice of law. No lawyers can understand your business better than you can. Lawyers are lawyers, not engineers, retailers, or chemists. As such, when they negotiate, they tend to pay attention to the legal issues they have been trained to spot, while overlooking the very real issues you are concerned with.

---

[15] It is not uncommon for lawyers to write and talk about this malaise. The law firm of Latham and Watkins, one of the nation's most prestigious firms, even did a study on the current state of the practice of law and issued what the California Lawyer termed "a scathing view" on the state of litigation in the United States. The Law Business: Some Lawyers Agree They're Part of the Problem, *California Lawyer*, June, 1992.

Never give a lawyer complete control

I know a number of law firms specializing in labor-management relations that refuse to represent any company in a union contract negotiation unless management gives them complete control and authority. They insist that management simply do what they say and stay out of the process. The results are almost always completely disastrous. These firms are famous for generating unnecessary conflicts that result in strikes, lock-outs, and long term bitterness between the workers and their management. And long after the law firm has collected its fee—and it's usually a doozie!—and departed, management is left picking up the pieces.

Whatever agreement you reach with the other side, *you* have to live with it, not your attorney. Remember, attorneys are consultants and nothing more. You make the final decisions. If the attorney starts making decisions without consulting you first, remind him who is in charge. If he still don't get it, hire another lawyer.

Returning a Lemon

You buy a product, paying your hard earned cash for it, only to discover you have wound up with a lemon. You complain, but the salesperson never returns your call. If you call one department, they refer you to another. The second department then refers you back to the first. Weeks pass without any resolution of the problem. Eventually, you give up. Rather than turn in the lemon, you suck on it. You feel cheated and defeated. So you do nothing more other than vow never to shop there again.

According to a study done by the U.S. Office of Consumer Affairs, one quarter of all purchases leave customers dissatisfied, but more than 70 percent of these disgruntled buyers do not complain, because they don't believe that protesting will accomplish anything.

This is disturbing for a number of reasons. First, commerce depends on a certain level of trust. If the trust between consumer and seller is lost, then buyers become reluctant to buy and sales are lost. And once a customer is lost, the potential for future sales to that customer is lost as well. The American automobile industry is learning this hard lesson and is now having to work to rebuild a reputation for quality and customer service that was lost during the sixties and seventies. The most successful retail outlets work hard to build and maintain customer satisfaction. Nordstroms department stores, for example, have built a reputation for customer service that seems to set the standard for the retail industry. My wife purchased a coat last year and decided a week later that she didn't like it. There was absolutely nothing wrong with the coat. She just didn't like it. They gave her a refund with no argument. The result of this customer-oriented approach is that my wife will buy at Nordstroms even if she knows that she could buy it cheaper somewhere else.

Second, with more and more companies focusing on customer service and switching to a total quality management ("TQM") system of internal management accounting, a growing number of companies *want* dissatisfied customers to complain. Their rationale is simple. If you don't complain, they lose a valuable opportunity to spot and correct defects or to otherwise improve the quality of the product. These complaints, called "customer feedback", are regularly tabulated and reviewed by the teams involved in production, product design, and research and development.

Unfortunately, not all sellers are concerned with customer satisfaction or use TQM in the production of their products or the rendering of their services. These businesspersons need to be dealt with firmly and immediately. However, don't jump to conclusions. Even when I have had problems with a vendor or salesperson, I rarely discover that they are being unethical. Corporations that do not handle complaints quickly are usually simply incompetent. Sometimes they are suffering from growing pains or they are simply understaffed. Whatever the situation, the following plan of action is appropriate for dealing with any intransigent or irresponsible salesperson or company.

- Act promptly. Don't delay. The longer you take to complain, the more likely they will fail to take your complaints seriously. Furthermore, you may find you are facing statutes of limitation that bar you from suing on your claim. For example, if you leave a valuable in a hotel or hospital safe deposit box when you check in, and those valuables are stolen or lost by the staff, in some states you must file suit within 60 days to collect.

- Collect and organize your facts before you begin. Be prepared to state, and support with canceled checks, sales slips, or whatever documentation you have, what you bought, when you bought it and what is wrong with it. Keep copies of all of the documents that you give the other side.

- Contact the salesperson who sold you the product first. Be polite. If you start off by accusing the other side of being deceptive or unethical, they will turn you off. A face-to-face encounter is always the best approach. However, this is not always possible, especially if you have purchased something by mail order. In that case, use the phone. State the facts. Avoid using emotional, inflammatory or accusatory language.

- Confirm your conversations with a letter. The confirming letter is an accurate record of what happened between you and the company. Be brief, polite, and to-the-point when you write this confirming letter. A good letter simply confirms the content of the conversation. Mail it immediately after the conversation has concluded. Return receipt requested mailing is not a bad idea in these situations. Of course, you should always keep a copy of the letter.

- Create deadlines. Never complete a conversation without setting a date by which they should respond to you. This keeps problems from being put off ad infinitum. Be reasonable in setting the deadline, but not overly generous. Ten days is generally the most that I will accept, although I have given longer deadlines if there is a compelling reason for it.

- Proceed up the organizational ladder. If the response from the salesperson is unsatisfactory, state politely but firmly that you will have to take this up with a superior. Ask who it is. If he refuses to tell you, send him a letter confirming this and then go right to the top.

- Call the manufacturer of the product. If the retailer doesn't act responsibly in handling your complaint, consider calling the manufacturer directly. Read the documentation that came with the product you purchased. There should be a corporate phone number on the pamphlet itself usually a 1-800 number. If you cannot find a phone number on the product packaging or manuals, go to your local library and look up the company in *Standard & Poors* or *Moody's*. You will find a phone number and address there. Ask if they have a customer service department. If they do, follow each step above in registering your complaint.

- If you used a credit card to make the purchase write to your credit card company. Carefully document the problems you have been having with the product and provide whatever written evidence you have. Send copies of documents, not the originals. Credit card companies are very helpful in assisting consumers who have purchased defective products. They will take up the matter directly with the retailer and credit your account accordingly. Frankly, this is sometimes the easiest solution.

Settle the Bad Cases Early and the Good Cases on the Courthouse Steps

Settle the Bad Cases Early . . .
The current Israeli ambassador to the UN, Abba Eban, once accused the Palestinians of never missing an opportunity to miss an opportunity. Palestinian demands that would have been easily achieved twenty years ago have now been lost to them forever because the Israeli govern-

ment keeps getting stronger, while the Palestinians keep getting weaker and more isolated. Before 1978, the Palestinians' demand was that Israel be replaced by a Palestinian state and that all Arab nations and the PLO withhold recognition from Israel. Even though the PLO was in the weaker negotiating position, it held to its position until the hard-line Likud coalition came into power and began to build hundreds of Jewish settlements on the West Bank. The likelihood that there will ever be a Palestinian state on the West Bank—something Israel could have previously conceded in exchange for Arab recognition during earlier times—is now remote, if not nonexistent.

There will come a time when you will try to unwind a sale and return an item that you have purchased. Your decision to try to negotiate the unwinding of a deal could be based on the fact that you were treated unfairly, or it could simply be because you made a bad decision to buy. When you know that your hand is weak, you are usually better advised to settle early, while the other side is facing a greater degree of uncertainty, rather than late in the game when the uncertainty they face is less. I have always been amazed at how trial lawyers with weak cases take hard line positions until it is too late to negotiate for anything. By the time the day for trial has arrived, the stronger side usually has little incentive or desire to make any significant concessions, and the opportunity for the weaker side to avoid disaster is lost.

. . . and the Good Cases on the Courthouse Steps

I am more than a little suspicious when people tell me they have the stronger side of a dispute. Fifty percent of the time, they are wrong. If you think you have the winning hand, be sure of it! Before doing anything, ask yourself this probing questions: "Why is the other side convinced I am wrong?" They must have *some* strong points in their favor. What are they?

If you are *still* sure of your position, relax. Be patient. Be very patient. There is nothing wrong with settling early if the terms make sense to you. If the other side presses you, however, take your time. As his alternatives disappear, and the day of judgment gets closer, the other side will fall under greater and greater pressure to settle in order to avoid disaster. In these circumstances, the other side's position usually collapses at the very end—the worst possible moment—forcing them to take whatever deal they can get.

How to Buy a Car in Less Than Five Minutes, Below Dealer Cost

Never buy a new car in a rural area or a small city.
Buy it in the biggest city that is within a seven hour drive instead. There are several reasons why automobiles are cheaper in large metropolitan areas than in lesser populated areas. First, there are more cars in metropolitan areas for the simple reason that there are more people. This means the average dealership's overhead cost per car is lower.

Second, there is a larger pool of cars for each dealership to draw from than there is in a lesser populated area. Even if a particular dealership does not have the make and model you want, they usually be able to execute a trade with another dealership that does have that particular car. If a particular color or option package is in short supply because of consumer demand, the price of that automobile tends to be tougher to negotiate. During particular demand periods, popular colors and option packages can be hard to find in the lower populated areas. This is rarely the case in places like Los Angeles, New York City, or Chicago.

Third, most car dealerships in smaller areas tend to have a higher fixed overhead than in more densely populated regions. Again, if your volume is larger, then the overhead can be spread over a greater number of sales. Since most overhead is a fixed cost, the buyer is always better off dealing with a larger dealership in a more highly populated area.

Only buy a new car between June and August.
Between June and August of every year, car dealers

are faced with a classic cash squeeze. First, they are required to purchase next year's models from the manufacturer. This means they have to come up with additional cash for this outlay. Second, approximately three months before the new models come out onto the showroom floor, the values of the existing models begin to depreciate. This depreciation in value is usually dramatic. Since the dealership's line of credit with the bank is collateralized by this inventory, the banks often demand that the dealership post additional cash to cover this shortfall ("compensating balances"). Because their inventory is depreciating at the same time they have to come up with additional cash for the manufacturer and their banker, dealerships are willing to sell cars for significantly less in order to generate cash flow. This means the dealership will often give their salespersons "bonuses for units sold" and introduce other buyer incentives, such as dealer and manufacturer rebates, to ensure that the "cash flows," even if the profit from the deal would be minimal or non-existent.

Determine what you should pay beforehand.

While this is not precise or completely accurate, my method it is a good "rule of thumb" approach to determining what to pay for a car between June and August. This pricing strategy was developed by myself and a banker who specializes in "flooring lines of credit," the loans made by banks to auto dealerships for the purchase of dealer inventory from the manufacturer.

Take the "base price" of the car and add to it the "base price" of the option package you want. This base price—the "dealer's cost" or invoice amount—is set forth in *Edmund's Catalog* or *Consumer Reports,* available at your local bookstore or library. Subtract from it all rebates offered by the manufacturer and the dealer. The result is the "off the lot price." To find out what the rebates are, call the dealership you are going to approach and ask them. They will tell you over the phone.

The "off the lot price" is what you should pay. Sales tax, license fees, and anything you need to pay to get the car off the lot should be included in this price.

Approach the dealer over the phone.

Let us assume you are interested in purchasing a 1992 Sable with a 941-A "preferred" option package with a blue leather interior and a white body. Go to the Yellow Pages for the largest metropolitan area within a seven hour drive. Call the first Lincoln Mercury dealer in the Yellow Pages and ask to speak to any salesperson. Tell her you are looking for a 1992 Mercury Sable and specify the model number you want. Tell her where you live and that you have an offer to buy this make and model of car for the price set forth above, but that you can't get the color scheme you want. If she has a white car with a blue leather interior, you will buy it from her. If not, you will buy the other car in your own area.

Because you can be disengaged from the process, and because it is not practical for the dealer to tell you to come into her office to negotiate, she is put in the uncomfortable position of either rejecting or accepting your offer. If the offer is above her bottom line, she will usually accept the offer.

After she agrees, fax her the following letter:

> This is to confirm our agreement of today wherein you agreed to sell me the following 1992 automobile (specify make, model number, color, and any other features you are interested in) for the following "off the lot" price (taxes, license and other fees included) $_____.
>
> I will bring a cashier's check with me tomorrow for this amount to close the sale. Please sign in the space provided below to confirm our understanding of this agreement.
>
> I agree to the foregoing.
>
> _____
>
> Name of Dealer

(*Note:* I am *not* giving legal advice here, just some tips on how to keep dealers off balance and at least embarrass them into being honest. See your lawyer if you want to know whether this is an enforceable agreement.)

Using the words "off the lot price" and mentioning the cashier's check you will be bringing prevents the dealer from adding on sales taxes, license fees, and other charges when you get there. Let her know you are dealing in "real money." That is the amount of cash you give to the dealer to get the car off the lot legally.

Make the trip.

Now fly to whatever metropolitan area you have selected (one way, of course) and buy your car. You will need plane fare, not much these days, and cab fare to the dealership, a good reason to pick a dealer near the airport. When you arrive, give them the cashier's check and drive your car home. Of course, the dealer will try to get you to buy expensive service agreements, extended warranties, and so on. Just say no.

If for any reason this approach doesn't work, simply turn to the Yellow Pages again and call the next dealer in that metropolitan area. There are dozens of them, and you will probably get the very same car off the same holding lot anyway!

Appendix A

Dealing with
Buyer's Remorse

Recently, a friend of mine visited my home in Northern California. While he was with us, we took him to a pottery store that sold a particular type and style of pottery he had been looking for. His excitement was readily apparent the moment he entered the store. After several hours of shopping and chatting with the store owner, who also shared his passion, he walked out with a vase he purchased for $250. Later on that night, he proudly unwrapped the vase and showed it to me. The very first thing I noticed about the vase was that it was chipped near the base. In all of his enthusiasm for the vase, he did not take notice of it until I pointed it out to him. Needless to say, I ruined his day, and I did not feel too good about it afterwards.

Sooner or later, each of us makes a bad purchase. Sometimes, we are the ones to blame. On other occasions, we are the victim of a hard sell or an outright fraudulent transaction. In any case, however, a bad purchasing decision is usually the result of one of two problems. Either we decide we have paid too much for something, or the product we purchased didn't live up to our expectations.

I Paid Too Much

There is only one way to verify if you paid too much. Check out the competition. Do some comparative pricing. If you did pay too much, determine if you paid just a little too much or if you got gouged. If you paid only slightly more than market, forget about it. Chalk it up to experience and realize you are now better prepared not to make the same mistake twice. On the other hand, if you got taken by the seller, see if the product is returnable. If it is, return it. If it isn't, revisit the seller and let them know you know you were taken. On occasion, the seller will adjust the price. In any case, you will have the satisfaction that comes with speaking your mind.

What if I can't afford to pay for it?

This is a bigger problem and one that requires prompt action. Most states have "cool down" laws for major purchases, such as automobiles and large consumer durable items. If you act promptly and return the item immediately, you may save yourself from a day in court and a bad credit rating. If you are unsure of your rights, see an attorney.

If you are stuck with the item, and you know that you cannot afford to make the payments consider the following:

Why did you purchase the item?

If you were pressured into the sale by a slick promotional campaign, see an attorney immediately. Most purchases can be "rescinded" by filing a small claims action or a lawsuit alleging that the sale was made under duress. If you purchased the item based on certain misrepresentations of fact that were made by the salesperson, you may be able to unwind the sale by alleging that it was made as the result of fraudulent misrepresentations of fact.

Can you negotiate a payment schedule you can live with?

If you are responsible for the purchase of the item, the next step is to contact the salesperson who sold it to you and let him know you cannot afford to pay for the product. It is probably a good idea to speak to someone in the store who has authority to deal with the situation such as a manager. Offer to return the product and unwind the transaction. Many sellers will unwind a transaction if they realize they are going to have difficulty collecting payment from you. If the product is now in a "used" condition, you may want to try to negotiate a payment schedule that both side's can live with.

Can you cut your losses?

At the very least, you may want to try to re-sell the product and at least cut your losses. This is especially important if you are strapped for cash. If you can resell the product for a price that approximates what you paid for it, great! If you are forced to sell at a discount, as is usually the case, at least you will be getting something back, rather than taking a total loss. This alternative should be used only after all other alternatives have been exhausted.

Why Did I Buy This?

This is the hard one. If you paid too much for something, you at least have the product. It may have been expensive, but most purchasers are still happy with the product and its capabilities. Buying something that you didn't need or want, however, is a true purchasing nightmare. Most people who fall into this category are impulse buyers. They get sucked into an enthusiastic sales pitch and, before they know it, they walk out of the office with something they absolutely don't need, such as a time share to a condo in Omaha, Nebraska. Only after they get home and the rest of their family asks them what in Sam Hill they had done, do they realize the mistake they made.

Before you throw the product into the dustbin or drop it off a balcony, however, it is probably a good idea to stop, cool down, and reassess your situation. Things are rarely as bad as they seem. Then ask yourself the following questions:

Is this product returnable?

One of my weaknesses is compact disks. I have a rather extensive collection of classical and jazz CDs. Occasionally, I will try out a CD from a new group I have never heard of before. As often as not, I am disappointed. The group may be good, but just not to my taste. For years, I would just put the CD up on the shelf and forget about it. Then, once a year, I would sell it, along with all my other bad CDs, to a used record shop at a steep discount. One day, a friend of mine watched me play a new CD I just purchased. When he saw I was disappointed in the music, he suggested I take it back. It turned out, he would always return any CD he didn't like within a few days of his purchase and get his money back. I learned the hard way that most products are returnable. The mere fact that the retailer doesn't advertise this may mean nothing. At the very least, most retailers are willing to let you trade in the product you bought for one that more closely meets your needs. Many give you your money back. In any case, you will never know until you ask.

Does this product have any value to me?

If the product isn't returnable, you then need to accurately assess the value the product does have for you. The idea here is to simply exploit the potential of the product in as creative a manner as possible, so the purchase isn't a total loss. When a friend of mine purchased a fax machine for his office, he discovered several weeks after the purchase that the machine did not have features he needed in order to properly submit bids on a construction project. He had to buy a new fax. He took the other fax and installed it in his home. It turned out to be one of the best decisions he ever made. He was able to review his employee's work on weekends, holidays, and in the early morning before he went to the office. Now he insists on having a fax at home.

Can I cut my losses?

It is a maxim of simple economics that you never look back at any decision. You only look forward. Assume for example that a film studio has spent 75 million dollars on a film that has still not been completed. The producers of the film know that it will cost another 10 million dollars to complete the film and that it will probably only gross 50 million dollars. The total loss on the film will be 35 million dollars. Should the studio complete the picture? The answer is yes. The 75 million dollars the studio has already spent is gone. It will never come back no matter what the studio does. The only question now is: should the studio spend an additional 10 million dollars to receive 50 million dollars? Cast in these terms, the answer is obvious.

Similarly, when you buy something you don't need or can't use, and you can't return it, don't panic. Try and look at the product creatively and objectively. Can the product be put to some use, notwithstanding its cost? Does the product have some utility that you can exploit? Can you re-sell the product and at least recover some of your losses? The answer to these questions is never a complete "no." Every product has some value or utility that can be exploited by someone. Your job is to discover that utility and exploit it at a maximum.

How Do I Get Out Of The Deal?

The first thing you must do is act promptly. Don't delay. If the vendor believes he is going to have a difficult time collecting money from you, he will be more likely to re-negotiate, or even unwind, the deal. Before you speak with the vendor, know your rights. If you have grounds for unwinding the deal, present him in a factual and confident manner. If persuasion doesn't work, and you have alternative courses of action open to you, let him know what these alternatives are. Offer some compromise if one is possible, such as a re-negotiated price or a payment schedule. In the final analysis, many vendors hate to re-negotiate price if they are convinced they can eventually collect from you.

In any case, try not to take it too seriously. If you reassess your position, you will probably find that you can afford to pay for the product if you have to and there are some valuable uses you can get out of the product. The things we buy are rarely useless and almost never impossible for us to pay for.

Appendix B

Dealing with Seller's Remorse

First, the Bad News

Five minutes after you sold your car to a person who answered your ad, you begin to have seller's remorse. Usually, this means you feel you should have gotten more for the automobile. Sometimes, you regret having departed with the automobile in the first place, at any price.

Seller's remorse is not as common as buyer's remorse, for the simple reason that the seller has usually had a longer period of time to think about the transaction before it has occurred. "Impulse selling" is not nearly as common as impulse buying. This is fortunate because it is much more difficult for sellers to unwind transactions than it is for buyers. There are some very persuasive reasons why.

Sellers have more information about the product

This is perhaps the best reason for holding a seller to the bargain, notwithstanding his subsequent remorse. Unlike buyers, sellers are more familiar with the product, obviously because they own it. The seller has had ample opportunity to familiarize himself with the product's strong points as well as with its weaknesses. He is more likely to know whether the product is defective, how durable it is and how practical it is for its designed use. As such, sellers are far less likely to impulsively sell an item. Furthermore, a seller is less likely to be defrauded in the sale of an asset, unless "funny money" is involved. In 11 years

of trying civil lawsuits, I have only rarely seen a seller successfully bring a suit for recission of a transaction. These
suits are more commonly won by buyers, especially when
the grounds of the suit are misrepresentation of fact by the
other side.

Possession is nine-tenths of the law

As old as this adage is, it represents a profound, fundamental truth about how our legal system works. Once
you give up possession of a product, it is usually very difficult to re-obtain custody of it. If, for example, you sell a car
to another individual and then sue to recover the automobile, there is a very strong likelihood the buyer will be per-
mitted to maintain possession of the car during the period
of the lawsuit. During this time, the asset will probably depreciate in value; it could even be damaged, lost, or stolen.
Traditionally, the possessor of an asset has a huge advantage in any suit over who has the lawful right of possession. This results in the seller constantly being pressured
to settle on terms that may ultimately benefit the buyer.
Conversely, once the buyer obtains possession, his incentive to settle tends to continue to dissipate over time.

Seller's remorse is the surest cure for buyer's remorse

If the buyer of a product is having second thoughts,
there is no surer way to reconfirm his confidence in his decision than to let him know that the seller is also having
second thoughts. This puts the seller on the horns of a
painful dilemma. If you tell the other side about your desire to unwind the transaction, will this have the perverse
result of hardening the buyer and steeling his resolve to
keep the product? On the other hand, if you say nothing
about your seller's remorse, there is the chance the buyer
may choose to approach you to unwind the transaction.
Your bargaining power will be stronger and you will be
able to get the item back and perhaps even make a few
bucks in the process. However, this doesn't happen all that
often. More commonly, if you remain silent, you may be
permanently surrendering the opportunity to unwind the
sale on any terms. The longer you delay trying to unwind
a transaction, the greater the possibility you will have per-

manently surrendered your right to do so, even if you were defrauded.

Now, the Good News

Although there is no question the seller is at a distinct disadvantage in trying to unwind a sale, your position is not entirely hopeless. There *are* certain things you can do.

Appeal to the buyer's better nature

A friend of mine discovered that his elderly mother had sold her automobile for a small fraction of what it was actually worth. Although the automobile was an older model, it only had 30,000 miles on it and it was in excellent condition. Furthermore, because she was living on a fixed income, she could not afford to purchase a replacement vehicle that would come anywhere near to what her existing car was worth. Obviously, she was at a severe disadvantage when she sold her automobile. Even though there was no question the transaction was valid and would stand up in court, there was an ethical dimension the law did not address. When the buyer purchased the car, he was fully aware of the fact that he was taking advantage of an elderly lady's ignorance of the true value of her car.

Rather than make threats, my friend decided to sit down with the buyer and explain his mother's dire financial predicament, as well as what the consequences would be to his mother if she lost the car. In short, he appealed to the buyer's conscience and to his better nature. After some discussion, the buyer agreed to unwind the transaction if my friend would pick up the costs incurred by the buyer when he purchased the car such as re-registering the vehicle, transfer taxes, and so on.

Most people are basically decent. Although, in some cases you may feel it is a long shot, it may not hurt to appeal to the other side's better nature when you want to unwind a sale. It may work. At the very least, it is worth a try.

Be prepared to pay for it

Generally, the seller does not unwind transactions without paying a price. Because he has very little leverage, he is usually required to offer the buyer an incentive to return the product. This is especially true if the buyer is satisfied with the purchase and not inclined to go back to square one. In short, if you want the product back, be prepared to pay for it. Whatever the premium is—a different product in place of the one you sold, paying more for the product than what you sold it for, or whatever—it will have to be attractive enough for the buyer to part with his gain.

"Funny money" and other related buyer's scams

Over the course of my practice of law, I have had a number of opportunities to sue buyers who had taken advantage of their sellers. In every case, the fraud that these buyers engaged in had more to do with the "funny money" that they paid their sellers on the close of the deal. Although I will not say that these cases are easy to win in every instance, they are the one exception to the general rule that sellers will not be able to unwind most sales. This is especially true if the buyer has more bargaining power than the seller and makes misrepresentations of fact in order to induce the seller to part with his asset.

The most common instance of buyer fraud, in my experience, is the "nothing down" real estate scam artist. This is, in my opinion, one of the most odious examples of fallen human nature in the late twentieth century. The "nothing down" buyer usually approaches someone who is elderly—usually a widow—who does not have an accurate understanding of what her home is worth. She may have purchased her home with her husband in the late fifties for $10,000. What she doesn't realize, and probably wouldn't believe, is that her home is now worth $200,000. Furthermore, she may have only recently suffered the loss of her spouse, or she may be contemplating a move. She may simply have come to trust the buyer, especially if he made a determined effort to ingratiate himself with her. At this point, the buyer makes a proposal to the seller. He will pay $100,000 *cash* for the house. And that isn't all! She will also receive an *additional* $75,000 promissory note which will be secured by the real estate, so there is no risk that the buyer will simply not make the payments on the note.

Of course, what the seller doesn't realize is that if she had simply sold her property in the traditional fashion, she would have received $200,000 cash instead of $100,000 in cash and $75,000 in paper. Furthermore, her $75,000 note will be subordinated to the $100,000 loan the buyer got from the bank. If the buyer defaults on the bank's $100,000, the seller will probably lose her $75,000 secured note. The result? She will have sold her home for half of what it was worth.

I have seen scams like this used to buy businesses, houses, automobiles, fine works of art, and valuable furniture. If you are ever victimized by one of these scam artists, see a lawyer, and see one quickly.

And in Any Case . . .

Quit torturing yourself

Recently, I saw a businessman interviewed who had just engaged in a bond issuance for his company in order to raise additional capital. Three days after the bonds had been placed in the market and sold, there had been a major swing in the market. As a result, if he had waited just three days before placing the bonds on the market, his interest rate would have been significantly lower than the one he got. Was he depressed? Absolutely not. In fact, he was quite pleased he raised the capitol he needed. I also got the impression that he was equally pleased that the process was over with. When a reporter asked him if he was happy with the deal he ended up with, he replied, "Of course. The deal was a good one." When the reporter mentioned that he could have done better, he responded: "I also could have done worse. You never look back."

Post-morteming a sale is one of the worst things you can do. Hindsight is twenty-twenty. The only question you should be concerned with is, did you accomplish the objectives you set out for yourself? If yes, then look forward. Don't look back. There will be other deals. Some of them will be better. Some worse. Take the long view, and don't worry so much. Life goes on.

Team Negotiating

Team negotiating seems to be occurring more and more often in the United States. Prior to the entry of the Japanese into our marketplace, it was rare to find teams negotiating with each other, except in highly structured settings where teams had traditionally operated, such as labor management negotiations.

The Japanese, on the other hand, have rarely negotiated alone. Their need for consensus, the importance of the group over the individual, and the comfort they feel in being part of a collective decision making process, as opposed to standing out from the pack, cause them to use teams almost exclusively in their negotiations. The result is that Americans are becoming more and more exposed to the strengths of team negotiating as we increase our business contacts with the Orient.

Team negotiating is really no different from one-on-one negotiating in its essentials. There are still two parties to the negotiations. The parties are just teams, not individuals. The importance of patience, a positive relationship, good listening and information gathering skills, an effective opening offer that is "anchored" to a viable target, a good bottom line analysis and justification for your proposals, are just as important with teams as they are with individuals.

The main difference between team negotiations and one-on-one negotiations is the need for collective decision making. With cultures that are more focused on the collective rather than the individual, group decision making is easy. Indeed, in societies such as Japan, where people are conditioned from early childhood to make decisions through the group rather than individually, team negotiating is almost second nature. Westerners, especially Americans, have little experience with this approach however, and tend to make glaring mistakes that can be very costly at the table.

To be effective, negotiating teams require coordination, integration, control, and a unity of purpose and vision that, sad to say, are rarely present in most of the teams I have watched or negotiated with. The purpose of this section is to provide some basic guidelines on how to achieve that level of integration and coordination a team requires.

What constitutes a team?

Team negotiating is any negotiation where there is more than one person on any side. If you and your spouse walk onto a car lot to purchase an automobile, you constitute a negotiating team whether you know it or not.

Should you ever negotiate against a team alone?

Never. Individuals are rarely able to handle the momentum and power teams have. Teams are usually able, through the sheer force of numbers, to control the agenda as well as the outcome of negotiations. Furthermore, individuals tend to lose patience when they negotiate against a team. As a result, they are more likely to be intimidated and be subjected to pressure tactics. Even if you feel you can hold your own against a team, you should rarely try. You will still *look* weak and the other side will be more inclined to try to use pressure or intimidation tactics. This puts a strain on your relationship. It also unnecessarily increases the other side's expectation of an easy deal.

What are the advantages to negotiating on a team?

Negotiating teams tend to be more thorough and creative. Teams tend to cover complicated issues with better scrutiny and with more patience than individuals. They generally provide a wider range of expertise and experience than individuals do. Teams also tend to make fewer mistakes than individuals do, because they have a larger pool of resources to draw on during and subsequent to negotiations.

Finally, teams are harder to intimidate or pressure. Indeed, because the responsibility for deadlock rarely falls on one individual, I would argue that teams are almost impossible to effectively intimidate or pressure.

What are the disadvantages of negotiating on a team?

They take longer. Exponentially longer. Teams have to caucus both in private and at the table. Consensus has to be achieved regularly. Sometimes the caucuses occur regularly and take a significant amount of time. Furthermore, everybody tends to need to have his say, both in caucus and at the table. If the team does not have a strong leader, it is very easy for "analysis paralysis" to set in. Indecisiveness tends to be the rule when people find they can avoid responsibility by deferring to the other members of the team.

Discipline can break down, and when it does, the result can be devastating. Whether it be as a result of a clash of egos or the over-enthusiasm of a member, there is no excuse for an out-of-control team member. Criticizing other team members, offering concessions that were not discussed in advance, or simply refusing to shut up can divide a team in minutes and destroy its effectiveness. It can also heighten the other side's expectations of an easy deal, create tension between the team members, cause critical information to be unnecessarily divulged, and give control to the other side. If you need a result quickly, try to negotiate one-on-one. If the other side intends to bring a team to the table, suggest that both sides send their most effective negotiator to negotiate one-on-one. If they insist on bringing a team, consider changing the deadline.

It is harder to create a positive relationship with the other side. Team negotiations tend to be more formal than one-on-one negotiations are. With individual negotiators, there is a greater opportunity for both sides to get to know each other personally and to establish some type of relationship. As a result, it is always a good idea for teams to meet socially at the start of important negotiations to establish some positive rapport. A reception, perhaps even a dinner, always makes a good start for negotiations.

The Profile Of An Effective Negotiating Team Includes The Following

- A strong leader.

- Clear consensus on what the team's negotiating position is and how they will provide rational justification for that position at the table.

- Every member of the team has an assigned role and knows how to specifically advance the team's position.

- The team focuses on the ultimate purpose of the negotiation rather than on personalities or egos.

- The team presents a united front to the other side. Disagreements, if any, are resolved in caucus, and ultimately by the team leader.

- The team has regularly rehearsed together.

- The team is highly disciplined when it comes to releasing information or taking positions at the negotiating table.

- The team members have a high degree of loyalty to the team, and not to any individual.

- There is group consensus going into negotiations as to what the opening offer will be, how it will be justified as a rational starting point for negotiations, and when it will be made.

- There is group consensus on what the negotiating target for the team will be.

- Whenever possible, there is group consensus on when to deadlock and when not to deadlock.

When should a team break from the table and go into caucus?

Constant caucusing can lead to unnecessary delays with the potential for something going wrong, something that could have been avoided. As such, teams should caucus only when there is a reason for doing so. If the team is properly prepared to negotiate, the need to caucus will tend to diminish. There are, however, certain occasions when it is absolutely necessary to break off and regroup.

When new information is received that may alter either side's position.

If you receive new information, it is always a good idea to break off and re-consider your negotiating position before going further. If the decision is fairly straightforward, a short caucus will be sufficient. If the new information is significant or requires further consideration, you may wish to ask for a recess and resume later.

In order to re-establish discipline among the members of the team.

If discipline breaks down among the team members, it is absolutely essential for a break to be taken. If the other side knows there is division on your negotiating team, there will be a greater probability that they will harden their position and/or seek to exploit the differences. Each member of a negotiating team should be willing to commit to the following understandings:

- All of the team members should "sing the same song" when taking positions or providing justification for those positions. If every negotiator has a different rationale for a particular position, the team loses momentum and does not appear to believe in its own arguments. Conversely, if all of the team members continually back each other and provide the same rationale for their position, their arguments will have greater weight with the other side. The opportunities for influencing the other side are increased.

- The team members must never contradict or argue with each other in front of the other side. This goes without saying and needs no explanation.

- The team members should back up each other. Never leave your colleague "swinging in the wind" when they are on the defensive. Support them immediately. If you don't, the other side will work to create division on your side of the table.

- Team members should not speak out of turn or

unnecessarily. There is nothing worse than "loose cannons" at the negotiating table. They tend to spill the beans early in the game, divulging information unnecessarily to the other side, backing off positions unnecessarily, and demoralizing their own team by their behavior. In the best teams, everyone has a role to play at the table. Each member knows when to speak and why. In any case, a team member who cannot be silent when required should be removed from the team. Again, a strong leader is helpful in this regard.

- Team members should speak for a purpose. Never say anything at the table unless you know what it is you are supposed to say and why you need to say it.

The other side has made an unexpected proposal

Certainly, if you receive a proposal from the other side that surprises you or is not what you expected to receive, you owe it to yourself, as well as to the other side, to break off and consider it.

The other side has asked a "hard" question that is difficult to answer

If the other side presents an argument you had never thought of before, do not try to respond to it before you have caucused. The worst thing you can do is respond immediately and find out you are wrong or that your response was flawed. Take a break. Discuss the other side's point with your colleagues, then formulate a response everyone on the team understands and is prepared to defend.

Before you deadlock

Never decide to deadlock without having one last caucus to see if a creative solution to the deadlock can be found. It is also a good idea to do a "reality check" and ask yourself whether you are truly deadlocking for a rational reason, or whether your ego is the cause of the problem. Take your time. You are about to make a decision that could have grave consequences. Once you have decided that you are deadlocked, be prepared to explain to the other side as a group why you are taking the position you are. The greater your justification and the better prepared you are to explain what it is, the better the chance the other side will re-evaluate their own position.

How Do You Conduct A Caucus?

The most important person during a caucus is the team leader.

The leader must maintain control

It is the leader's responsibility to maintain the group's focus and to make the ultimate decisions for the group. The leader must also be sure that the group is properly prepared before they return to the table and that everyone understands the position of the team thoroughly. In the event of dissension among members of the team, the leader should listen to everybody's input, then make a decision. That decision should settle the matter. As a practical matter, it would be helpful if the leader had some institutional status, such as seniority among the team members, or have a great deal of respect from the other members.

Explain why the caucus has been called.

Whoever called the caucus should immediately inform the other members why. State your reason clearly and succinctly. Be specific.

Don't drift off the subject

This is where leadership comes into play. If the team gets sidetracked, remind them of the real issue to be resolved and give them a reality check. Subject drift causes caucuses to go into overtime and leaves the critical issues unresolved. It also tends to create unnecessary dissension and confusion among the team.

Allow each side to state their opinion

Don't allow protracted argumentation. When this occurs, there is a tendency for each side to want to get in the last word. Feelings get hurt, sides harden, and nothing gets resolved. Encourage all members to state opinions without reacting to the opinions of the other members.

Keep the discussion focused on best alternatives

This is perhaps the hardest lesson to learn. Negotiation is a pressure cooker. Egos get involved. Personalities tend to express themselves in a less than favorable light. As such, there is a tendency for teams to go into caucus and work themselves up into a frenzy because of something the other side has or has not done. Objectivity is lost, and mistakes are inevitably made that have to be repaired later. By simply focusing on your existing alternatives, your decisions tend to be more objective and less emotional. All members of the team tend to give more constructive, focused, and intelligent input when they use this approach to decision making.

Establish consensus on your next move

As a group, you should come out of a caucus with complete consensus on what the team's next move is going to be and why. It is also helpful to reinforce what the team's negotiating goal or target is and where the negotiations are in relation to that target. Each team member should know what the team's justification will be for its next position, in order that there will be complete unanimity on your side at the table. This will help give you control and momentum. It will also make your team look and act more confident.

Negotiating by Telephone

It is the rare negotiator who doesn't make agreements over the telephone. And it is a very rare breed of negotiator, indeed, who will not be making more and more deals by telephone as our society progresses into the information age. This should surprise nobody. As time becomes more valuable, and as the demands of our various professions increase, telephone negotiating is increasingly becoming the norm, rather than the exception.

In the not too distant past, it was the conventional wisdom that making deals by telephone was, at best, a necessary evil, and, at worst, a short-cut to broken agreements and the courthouse. Rarely anybody subscribes to this theory anymore. Time is simply too precious to drop everything, drive across town, sit in someone's reception room for 20 minutes, then meet with them in order to close a deal. If all of us did this for every deal we negotiated, we would rarely have time for anything else.

Fax machines, e-mail, Federal Express, conference calls, communicating through the Internet, and tele-conferencing have changed our attitudes towards the lowly telephone. Telephone conversations can be immediately followed up in writing and in person. Written contracts can be reviewed by fax within minutes of being drafted. In construction contracts, the fax machine has revolutionized the manner in which bids are submitted to the prime contractor by its potential sub-contractors on "bid day." It is also possible for all sides to review competitive bids within minutes of being submitted to the public agency that solicited them. Indeed, telephone negotiating is even becoming more prevalent among salespersons, the one group of negotiators for whom the "sales call" has, in the past, been sacrosanct.

While there are still drawbacks to negotiating by telephone, they have been considerably lessened by the new technologies that are telephone related, especially the fax and e-mail. Traditionally, negotiators preferred not to negotiate over the telephone for the following reasons:

Conversations are more likely to be misunderstood because they take less time

In this sense, the strength of a telephone is also its weakness. When people talk over the telephone, they tend to take less time communicating than they would in person. Hellos and good-byes are less prolonged. Small talk tends to be more perfunctory and briefer. Even the substantive portion of conversations is faster and more to the point. Of course, there is much to be said for this when time is money in your business. You can speak to more people in a day, and accomplish more than you could in person in a week. The drawback is, there is a greater likelihood the parties will misunderstand each other in a telephone conversation than in a face-to-face meeting for the simple reason that less time is spent saying what you have to say over the telephone.

Conversations are more likely to be misunderstood because they are deprived of the "context" of body language

Another reason telephone conversations are more likely to be misconstrued is because body language is filtered out. As a result, the nuances that are ordinarily communicated through smiles, hand gestures, shrugs, frowns, or a simple twitch of the eyebrow is lost. Anthropologists call this body language "context," and it constitutes a significant portion of the way we communicate. When this "context" is filtered out of our conversations, the likelihood of misunderstandings is increased. People tend to take the meaning of each other's words more literally in a telephone conversation than they do in person. Thus, there is a greater likelihood the parties will misunderstand each other. This is especially true in "high context" societies, such as Japan, where seating arrangements, body language, and the subtle nuances of highly refined behavior take on an even greater importance. When dealing with these societies, there is often no substitute for a face-to-face meeting.

The party on the receiving end of the telephone call usually has had no opportunity to prepare

As has already been noted in this book, preparation is your greatest single edge in any negotiation. Those negotiators who "make it up as they go along" are more likely to make mistakes during the negotiation process that are permanently injurious, sometimes fatally so, to their long-term interests.

There is a greater likelihood that one party will "walk out"

One of the ironies of telephone negotiations is that it is more likely to create heated disputes between the parties than face-to-face negotiations. This is because it is harder to get angry with someone and express it face-to-face than when there is a barrier of some sort. When we meet someone in person, we tend to be more polite and more easily embarrassed by anti-social behavior than when we talk to them over the telephone. As such, most people find it easier to blow up and hang up on you on the telephone than to physically walk out of a negotiation.

Telephone conversations are easy to terminate

Actually, this can be both a strength and a weakness. Because most people dislike long telephone conversations, and dislike negotiating even more, it is usually easier to break off a conversation during a lull with a promise to call them back later than it is if you are negotiating face-to-face. For one thing, face-to-face negotiations are set up only with a certain amount of difficulty. As such, people expect problems to actually be resolved during these meetings. If the face-to-face meeting concludes without the major problems being resolved, people tend to leave the meeting feeling they have wasted their time. Second, because it is usually easier to reschedule a telephone conversation than it is to reschedule a face-to-face meeting, people feel safer terminating phone calls prematurely.

Telephone calls are difficult to restart

Conversely, once your telephone conversation has been terminated, it is easier for the other side to put off talking to you again. Meetings have to be canceled. Telephone calls can simply be avoided (the "tell him I'm not in" syndrome). If you are anxious to see the matter between you and the other side resolved, this can be a source of continual frustration for you. And when you finally do re-establish contact, there is a greater likelihood there will be disagreements between you and the other side as to where you left matters when you concluded your prior conversation. Of course, all of this may be to your advantage if you wish to delay or terminate negotiations gently. In that case, you will find it easier doing so over the telephone than you will in person.

It can be more difficult to concentrate

People in our office or home tend to give us less privacy when we are on the phone than when we are in a meeting. This is natural and easily understood. Meetings tend to have an aura of seriousness around them that creates a sense of respect. The same people who will gleefully shove letters in our face when we are on the phone wouldn't dare enter our office if we were meeting the same person for the same reason. Similarly, if you were in a meeting and someone popped into your office to say "hello," your secretary would be a lot more reticent about interrupting your meeting than if you received an incoming call while you were on the line with the same person.

Tips for Negotiating by Telephone

1. Be prepared. Never answer an incoming call you are not prepared for before you think about what you are going to do. If you are not sure, beg off. An easy way to do this is to tell the other side you are tied up at the moment but you would like to call

them back. Set up a specific time and date for your return call. People generally dislike being strung along. Then, before you return their call, make a list of issues you want to address, questions you want to ask, trial balloons you would like to float in their direction, notes about your bottom line, and general notes about how you intend to provide rational justification for your next position.

2. Prevent potential distractions before you begin. Do not try to negotiate with the other side unless you are prepared to give the discussions your full and complete attention. Before you make the return call, it is a good idea to close the door to your office. Let everyone know, in no uncertain terms, that you are not to be disturbed. Wrap up whatever it is that you are doing, clear off your desk, and free your mind from the other non-related issues you have been dealing with. Then, and only then, make your call.

3. Open with small talk. It is a good idea to commence your conversation with a certain amount of low-risk small talk. This accomplishes two things. First, it creates a positive atmosphere for negotiations and helps lower the other side's shield and gets their sword on the table. Second, it allows you to get a handle on what their voice and intonation sound like when they are relaxed and un-threatened. This can be used as a benchmark for determining how they are reacting to your various proposals when you are in the midst of your substantive discussions with them.

4. Take notes. It is harder to remember the various points that are being made by the other side when you are talking on the telephone. As we have already noted, telephone negotiations lack the context of body language and tend to invite interruptions, on their side of the phone as well as on yours. This means that telephone conversations are more likely to be disjointed and abbreviated.

By taking notes, you not only help yourself to keep focus, but you have a valuable record of what was said and what, if anything, was accomplished by the conversation.

5. Slow it down! Be clear and precise. Slow down the pace of the conversation. Get in the habit of repeating your main points and your justification for them. Be sure you are speaking clearly and for a purpose. Never assume the other side understands what it is you are getting at. In fact, unless you are absolutely clear that such is the case, it is probably a good idea to assume just the opposite! Always work from notes, including the checklist of items you wanted to cover that was prepared before you made your telephone call. This will eliminate the tendency of both parties to gloss over or completely forget important points that need to be covered thoroughly.

6. Confirm their position by restating it in the light most favorable to them, without agreeing if you disagree. Never assume you understand their position until you have restated it better than they could, while at the same time driving home the point you do not necessarily agree. By giving them this feedback early in the conversation and frequently thereafter, you avoid costly misunderstandings that can complicate negotiations for both of you.

7. When suspending negotiations, set up a telephone appointment for the next call. Confirm it in writing as soon as possible. This will help to lessen the likelihood that the other side will get the impression you are stringing them along. It will also make it easier for you to re-establish contact later, and keep them from stringing *you* along.

8. Follow up each phone call with a confirming letter. The confirming letter should be drafted immediately after the telephone conversation, regardless of whether you have reached agreement on sub-

stantive issues or not. It should also be mailed or faxed, preferably both, to the other side immediately. Confirming letters accomplish two valuable things. First, they prevent misunderstandings growing into disputes, because they call the misunderstanding to both parties' attention before the parties act on them. Second, confirming letters can be used in court to support your position if there is a subsequent dispute over what was, or was not, agreed to by the parties.

Bibliography

Aumann, Robert J. "Agreeing to Disagree." *Annals of Statistics* (1976), 4: 1236-1239.

Axelrod, Robert. "Conflict of Interest: An Axiomatic Approach." *Journal of Conflict Resolution* (1967), 11: 87-8\99.

Bacow, Lawrence and Michael Wheeler. *Environmental Dispute Resolution.* Plenum Press, New York, NY, 1984.

Bazerman, Max H. "Negotiator Judgment." *American Behavioral Scientist* (1983), 27: 211-228.

Beckman, N. *Negotiations.* Lexington Books, Lexington, MA, 1977.

Callieres, Francois De. *On the Manner of Negotiating with Princes*, translated by A.F. Whyte. Houghton Mifflin, Boston, MA, 1919.

Cohen, Herb. *You Can Negotiate Anything.* Lyle Stuart, Secaucus, NJ, 1980.

Condlin, Robert J. "Cases on Both Sides: Patterns of Argument in Legal Dispute-Negotiation." *The Maryland Law Review*, (1985) 44, 1: 65-136.

Crawford, Vincent P. "A Theory of Disagreement in Bargaining." *Econometrica* (1982), 50: 607-637.

Crawford, Vincent P. "Compulsory Arbitration, Arbitral Risk and Negotiated Settlements: A Case Study in Bargaining Under Imperfect Information." *Review of Economic Studies* (1982), 49: 69-82.

Deutsch, Morton. *The Resolution of Conflict: Constructive and Destructive Processes*. Yale University Press, New Haven, CT, 1977.

Deutsch, Morton and R.M. Kraus. "Studies of Interpersonal Bargaining." *Journal of Conflict Resolution* (1962), 6: 52-76.

Dunlop, J.T. *Wage Determination Under Trade Unions*. Augustus Kelley Press, New York, NY, 1980.

Dunlop, J.T. *Dispute Resolution: Negotiation and Consensus Building*. Auburon House, Dover, MA, 1984.

Emerson, R.M. "Power Dependance Relations." *American Sociological Review* (1961), 27: 31-40.

Faber, Mike and Roland Brown. "Changing the Rules of the Game: Political Risk, Instability and Fair Play in Mineral Concession Contracts." *Third World Quarterly* (1980), 2: 100-120.

Fayerweather, John and Ashook Kapoor. *Strategy and Negotiation for the International Corporation*. Ballinger, Cambridge, MA, 1976.

Fisher, Roger. *International Conflict and Behavioral Science: The Craigville Papers*. Basic Books, New York, NY, 1964.

Fisher, Roger. "What About Negotiation as a Specialty?" *American Bar Association Journal* (1983), 69: 1221-1224.

Fisher, Roger and William Ury. *Getting to Yes: Negotiating Agreements Without Giving In*. Houghton Mifflin, Boston, MA, 1981.

Geanakoplos, John and Heraklis Polemarchakis. "We Can't Disagree Forever." *Journal of Economic Theory* (1982), 26: 192-200.

Goldberg, S.B., E.D. Green, and F.E.A. Sander. *Dispute Resolution*. Little Brown Publishers, Boston, MA, 1985.

Greenhalgh, L. and S.A. Neslin. "Cojoint Analysis of Negotiator Preferences." *Journal of Conflict Resolution* (1981), 25: 301-327.

Gulliver, P.H. *Disputes and Negotiations: A Cross Cultural Perspective.* Academic Press, New York, NY, 1979.

Hall, Edward. *The Silent Language.* Doubleday, New York, NY, 1959.

Hall, Edward. "The Silent Language in Overseas Business." *Harvard Business Review* (1960), May-June.

Hofstadter, Douglas. "Metamagical Themas: Computer Tournaments of the Prisoner's Dilemma Suggest How Cooperation Evolves." *Scientific American.* May 1983.

Hofstadter, Douglas. *How Nations Negotiate.* Harper & Rowe, New York, NY 1964.

Lax, David A. "Optimal Search in Negotiation Analysis." *Journal of Conflict Resolution* (1985), 3: 456-472.

Lax, David A. and James K. Sebenius. "Insecure Contracts and Resource Development." *Public Policy.* (1981), 29: 417-436.

Lax, David A. and James K. Sebenius. "Negotiating Through an Agent." Harvard Business School Working Paper, 83-87, 1983.

Lax, David A. and James K. Sebenius. "The Power of Alternatives and the Limits to Negotiation." *Negotiation Journal* (1985), 1: 163-179.

Lewicki, Roy J. and Joseph A. Litterer. *Negotiation.* Irwin Press, Homewood, IL, 1985.

Malouf, Michael W.K. and Alvin E. Roth, "Disagreement in Bargaining: An Experimental Approach." *Journal of Conflict Resolution* (1981).

Pen, J. "A General Theory of Bargaining." *The American Economic Review* (1952).

Peters, Edward. *Strategy and Tactics in Labor Negotiations.* National Foreman's Institute, New London, CT, 1955.

Pruitt, Dean G. *Negotiation Behavior.* Academic Press, New York, NY 1981.

Pruitt, Dean G. "Strategic Choice in Negotiation." *American Behavioral Scientist* (1983).

Pruitt, Dean G. *The Art and Science of Negotiation.* Harvard University Press-Belknap Press, Cambridge, MA, 1982.

Pruitt, Dean G. "Post-settlement Settlements." *Negotiation Journal*, (1985), 1: 9-12.

Rapoport, A. and A.M. Chammah. *Prisoner's Dilemma.* University of Michigan Press, Ann Arbor, 1965.

Roth, Alvin. *Axiomatic Models of Bargaining.* Springer Press, Berlin, 1979.

Salter, Malcolm. "Negotiating Corporate Strategy in Politically Salient Industries." Harvard Business School Working Paper 84-07, 1984.

Sawyer, Jack and Harold Guetzkow. "Bargaining and Negotiations in International Relations." Contained in Herbert C. Kelman's *International Behavior: A Social-Psychological Analysis.* Holt, Rinehart & Winston, New York, NY, 1965.

Strauss, Anselm L. *Negotiations: Varieties, Contexts, Processes and Social Order.* Jossey-Bass, San Francisco, 1978.

Tedeschi, J.T., R.B. Schlenker and T.V. Bonoma. *Conflict, Power and Games: The Experimental Study of Interpersonal Relations.* Aldine Publishers, Chicago, IL, 1973.

Tedeschi, J.T., R.B. Schlenker and T.V. Bonoma. *A Behavioral Theory of Labor Negotiations.* McGraw Hill, New York, NY, 1965.

Williams, G.R. *Legal Negotiations and Settlement.* West Publishing Company, St. Paul, MN, 1983.

Wriggens, W. *The Negotiation Process: Theories and Applications*. Sage Press, Beverly Hills, CA, 1978.

Wriggens, W. and Maureen Berman. *The Practical Negotiator*. Yale University Press, New Haven, CT, 1982.

Index

About the Author

LEO P. REILLY is a California lawyer and a national lecturer and trainer in negotiation skills. As an attorney specializing in negotiation strategy, he provides consulting services to his corporate and government clients on how to negotiate specific contracts. His educational background includes a Master's Degree in International Law from the University of London, and a Master's Degree in Business Taxation from the University of Southern California. He has practiced law in California since 1978.

Since 1984, Leo Reilly has presented over 2,500 seminars, televised closed network presentations, and delivered public speeches on the subject of negotiation. His clients include U.S. Government agencies, universities, professional organizations, and over 50 Fortune 500 companies. They include Tandem Computers, KLA Instruments, Adobe Systems, Fujitsu Corporation, Toyota of America, MCA Universal Studios, Bechtel Corporation, Bank of America, NASA, Whirlpool Corporation, ASK Computers, Silicon Graphics Corporation, the Department of Defense, the Veterans Administration, the U.S. Air Force, the U.S. Navy, the Treasury Department, the Internal Revenue Service, the American Chemical Society, the U.S. Army Corps of Engineers, the State of Massachusetts, the City of Los Angeles, the University of California, and many more. Leo Reilly regularly conducts on-site training and can be reached at 1-800-925-EDGE (3343).